Famili

"The family has no beginning and no end. In the family reside the deeds of the past, the breath of the present, and the yearning of the future. The family is the constant of the human universe-it is like the sky-something that has been and will always be."

George W. Baley,
US ambassador to the Republic of Gambia

In remembrance of the times we've shared. Joyce Brown

Note for Librarians: A cataloguing record for this book is available from Library and Archives Canada at www.collectionscanada.ca/amicus/index-e.html
ISBN 1-4120-5166-5

Printed in Victoria, BC, Canada. Printed on paper with minimum 30% recycled fibre. Trafford's print shop runs on "green energy" from solar, wind and other environmentally-friendly power sources.

TRAFFORD
PUBLISHING™
Offices in Canada, USA, Ireland and UK
This book was published *on-demand* in cooperation with Trafford Publishing. On-demand publishing is a unique process and service of making a book available for retail sale to the public taking advantage of on-demand manufacturing and Internet marketing. On-demand publishing includes promotions, retail sales, manufacturing, order fulfilment, accounting and collecting royalties on behalf of the author.

Book sales for North America and international:
Trafford Publishing, 6E–2333 Government St.,
Victoria, BC V8T 4P4 CANADA
phone 250 383 6864 (toll-free 1 888 232 4444)
fax 250 383 6804; email to orders@trafford.com
Book sales in Europe:
Trafford Publishing (UK) Limited, 9 Park End Street, 2nd Floor
Oxford, UK OXI IHH UNITED KINGDOM
phone 44 (0)1865 722 113 (local rate 0845 230 9601)
facsimile 44 (0)1865 722 868; info.uk@trafford.com
Order online at:
trafford.com/05-0061

10 9 8 7 6 5 4 3

Dedication

When I first began to teach school, a student asked me, "Miss McDonald, what was it like to grow up in the olden days? You know, when there were dinosaurs on the earth." I am, perhaps, not that old, but certainly I have seen many changes in the last seventy years. I dedicate this book to my children, my grandchildren and my great-grandchildren. I hope it will give them an appreciation of what life was like in the olden days.

Acknowledgements

I would like to thank the editors of this book:

Tom Brown, the expert, who taught me some of his computer tricks. It would have been easier to complete this work if I were a better student. You did your best, Tom.

Diane Rutledge, thank you for keeping the time line logical, the pictures in their correct places and for keeping me on task.

Sara Rutledge, thank you for applying your journalism knowledge to this work. I hope this experience will not deter you from continuing your career as an editor.

I take responsibility for any errors that remain. It is my story and I am sticking to it!

Table of Contents

Families Are Forever 1
Dedication 3
Acknowledgements 4
Table of Contents 5
A Full House 1930-1936 1
Playtime 15
Pets We Loved 23
Health and Medical Care 27
Clothing 31
School Days in Abbotsford 1936-1948 35
Special Occasions 45
Job Opportunities 49
The War Years 1939-1945 55
Normal School 1948-1949 63
Teaching in Langley 1949-1952 69
Courtship and Marriage 75
Life on the Farm 1951-1956 85
Penticton 1956-1957 101
Mt. Lehman 1957-1959 109
Aldergrove 1959-1961 119
Shearwater 1961-1963 125
Ocean Falls 1963-1968 153
Bella Coola 1968-1969 173
Back to Ocean Falls 1969-1974 183
Victoria 1974-1986 201
Fort McMurray 1986-1995 217
Mississauga 1995-1997 231
Saskatoon 1997 - 2002 241
So Far 247
A Letter to My Family 248
The Family Tree – So Far 251
The Family Pictures 257

A Full House
1930-1936

In 1930, my father, Harry McDonald, managed a lumberyard in Riceton, Saskatchewan. With my imminent arrival just days away, my parents, Harry and Bessie McDonald, set out for Kisbey, SK.

My great aunt Jane Smith, or Auntie, as we called her, had trained as a mid-wife in Derby, England. She came to Canada in 1916 to be near her sister, Emma Pridmore, my grandmother. As there were no hospitals in Riceton or Kisbey where Auntie lived, she set aside one room in her house as a maternity ward. Usually a pregnant woman stayed there for about two weeks before her due date to wait her baby's arrival. The outlying farms were often many miles from Kisbey and the roads were crude and frequently impassable. Deep ruts and sticky gumbo mud formed after a rain or during break-up, causing the wagons and cars either to slide off the road or to stick in the mud. No roads had pavement.

Dad had a car, a rarity in the thirties. My parents drove from Riceton to Kisbey to await my delivery. Fathers in those days did not witness childbirth so dad was relegated to the basement to keep the furnace stoked all night. It is still cold on the prairies in early May. Mother had a very long and difficult labour, as I was a breech birth. No doubt being born bottom first accounts, at least in part, for my sometimes contrary or perverse perception of the world about me. Auntie's account book has a brief note that says, "May 8, 1930. Received from Harry McDonald $5 for delivery of a girl 6 pounds 4 ounces."

Mother and Dad had eloped to Regina, SK, May 5, 1929 where a Baptist minister married them. Before my birth, a Catholic priest remarried my parents. This assured my grandparents that I was a legitimate child. Grandpa and Grandma McDonald did not believe my parent's original marriage was legal in the eyes of the

1

church. On the way home from my birth in Kisbey, my parents stopped at Forget, SK where a priest baptised me.

Mary Joyce McDonald - First Christmas

June 30 1931, Auntie also delivered my brother, Ian Alexander, in her home in Kisbey. By this time, Saskatchewan was in the midst of the Great Depression. Huge dust storms ravaged the farmland removing the topsoil in clouds of dust that seeped into the houses and piled up on the fence lines. Often the sun was obscured. With the drought came hordes of grasshoppers that cleaned off whatever grain tried to grow. Auntie said that in the Kisbey area, children beginning Grade One in school had never seen rain in their lives.

The economy was devastated. Farmers vacated their land as more and more banks foreclosed on mortgages. Businesses could not operate without sales from the farmers. No one was buying lumber to build houses and barns. My Dad lost his job, as did thousands of others.

Without any prospects on the prairies, with no hope for the future, and two babies to feed, my parents moved to Abbotsford, B.C., to live with Dad's parents, Duncan and Elsie McDonald. Economically, conditions were little better in the Fraser Valley, but Grandpa and Grandma were generous and shared what they had. They still had eight children living at home. One daughter,

2

Mary, had died of a brain tumour at age eighteen and my Uncle Duncan had "hit the rails".

During the Depression, thousands of young men jumped on the trains, often in empty boxcars or on the roofs of the rail cars, crossing Canada looking for work. Little employment was available so these men became tramps stopping at houses and begging for food in exchange for work doing chores or for the opportunity to sleep in a farmer's barn. There was no stigma attached to this begging and people felt no fear of these young men as they tried to survive. No unemployment insurance or other safety nets were available to people who lost their jobs. Tramps would identify houses that offered food by placing marks on the gates. We must have had such a mark on our gate as Mother often fed tramps as they passed by. I am sure she hoped others were feeding my dad's brother who was in the same position.

My grandpa had a house built on 20 acres of land on the Ware Road in Abbotsford, adjoining 20 acres belonging to his brother, Jim McDonald. We, as children, loved to walk across Grandpa's fields and over the stile to Uncle Jim's house. Uncle Jim had many things Grandpa did not have: a cream separator, a butter churn, a huge grindstone, and best of all, a white horse. I realize now that all those interesting items actually meant much hard work.

Grandpa's house is still standing, remodelled and beautifully landscaped. Uncle Jim's house on the Marshall Road has had little, if any, maintenance work done, and, today appears ramshackle and forlorn. Surrounding it are overgrown shrubs and gnarled, unpruned fruit trees. Abbotsford High School and many modern homes now occupy the land once owned by the two McDonald brothers.

Grandpa did not enjoy farming as he had been a businessman, but he kept a cow and had a large vegetable garden to feed the 10 in their family (Aunt Elsie, then a teenager, and seven boys ranging down to age seven) Now this number was augmented by our four extra.

Mother told of the hardships of this first winter. When the ground was frozen, she and Elsie went out in the garden and tried to find

3

a carrot or potato missed during the harvest that could go into the soup pot. The children had hardly enough clothes to go around. The boys would often have to stay in bed when their pants were washed because they had only one pair. I remember my Grandma crying as she told about Christmases with nothing for any child. On one occasion, someone gave my parents a small barrel of pickled herring, which was their main protein for that winter. No one enjoyed this fish and my parents never purchased or ate herring again, but the family survived and was grateful.

Grandpa, dad and his younger brothers cut wood and delivered it for 75 cents a cord. Dad also tried to earn money in other ways. He would pedal his bicycle across Sumas Prairie trying to sell insurance to the local farmers. He delivered bread; he would take labouring jobs for 25 cents a day.

There were few if any teaching jobs. Occasionally Dad got a few days substitute teaching. Eventually this part-time work grew into a permanent position. Dad taught grade seven at Abbotsford Elementary School and later became its vice-principal.

However, my grandparents could not meet the payments on their house and the bank foreclosed. They moved to Greenwood in the Kootenays. Greenwood was virtually a ghost town, vacated after the mining boom of the early 1900's. During WW2, Greenwood became the home of many Japanese deported from the West Coast.

Eventually my dad found a house to rent across the highway from the Hindu Temple. We were living in this house when, on August 10, 1932 another son, Donald Bain McDonald, was born.

The next year, mother's sister, Joyce, came to visit. She wrote home that there were not two but three babies. My parents had not told the Pridmore family about Donald, as they did not want them to worry further about the hard times in Abbotsford.

Mother holding Donald with Ian in the stump - 1934

A highlight of Aunt Joyce's visit was, for me, a trip down town to a restaurant for a soda. I did not know, as a four year old, that there were such treats. When I got home, I told my Mother excitedly that I had a soda and drank it with knitting needles. One summer day, Dad borrowed a car to take Uncle Jim and Aunt Gertrude to Vancouver to get eyeglasses. Their daughter, Margaret, took care of the children. For an outing, we walked downtown. On our way home, a friend of Dad's, Harvey Henderson, picked us up in his car and brought us to our house. Flames enveloped the house. We stood and watched as it was destroyed. An old trunk filled with papers the children used to colour was all that was saved. Mother spoke of a wedding gift; a complete dinner set of Limoge china, which went up in smoke. When my parents arrived home that night, all that remained in our yard was the smouldering remains of our house. Until they returned to Uncle Jim's house, they had no idea if their children were alive or dead.

While staying at Uncle Jim's, Ian dropped an iron on his foot causing serious damage to his big toe. I was impressed because

5

his foot was soaked in a solution containing gentian violet, which dyed his foot a bright purple up to the high water mark.

Joyce, Donald & Ian – 1934

In a few weeks, Dad found a small house to rent some distance from town on the McKenzie Road. Under the back step was a huge pile of old tins and bottles. Donnie climbed underneath the stoop and drank from several of these containers. It was very exciting to watch the panic and the machinations of my parents as they did what parents do to induce vomiting and save Donnie's life. It was too expensive to go to the doctor so people learned to look after themselves, except for the most serious illnesses.

We were excited to find out there was a skunk living under this porch. It was even more comfortable once mother and dad removed the bottles and other junk. The compelling odour wafting through the bedroom windows first attracted our attention. Later we thought how cute he was, stamping his little feet and giving off other warning signs. Luckily, our parents saw what was going on and pulled us quickly out of his path. Later, they lured him away with a saucer of milk.

Not long afterward, we moved to the house on the Old Yale Road, which became our family home until after my dad retired. When the sawmill on Mill Lake closed, the company houses were sold and my parents acquired one for a few hundred dollars. I remember taking the monthly payments of ten dollars to the company office.

Michael was born September 15, 1934. I remember how cute he was when Mother brought him home. It was a surprise to have a brother with brown hair and eyes after two very blond brothers. The nurse in the hospital told Mother he looked like a Michael and that is how he got his name. This was the origin of the Michaels and Michelles in our family.

Joyce, Donald & Ian

In looking back, I wonder how we managed to live in such a small house, though it did not seem small at the time and was typical of our community. It was 28 feet square, divided into four rooms, with the two bedrooms smaller than the kitchen and living room.

Our parent's room contained a double bed, a dresser, and a crib for the baby. There was a closet off one end of the room. In the other bedroom were two single beds and a dresser. There was one closet about five feet long that held all the children's clothes.

In the living room were a large, square oak table and several wooden chairs. Beside one chair was a small end table. There was also a wood heater standing on a decorated tin mat. The stovepipe extended about a foot from the wall to minimize the danger of fire. The children always dressed around the heater in the winter. I think my brothers likely still have scars on their bottoms from backing into the heater as they were dressing. Because no houses had insulation, they were very cold at night. There was often frost on the windows and you could see your breath in the cold morning air.

7

Each room had one electric light bulb hanging from the centre of the ceiling. A chain dangling from the fixture lit the bulb. I do not remember any outlets except one in the kitchen and one in the living room. We felt lucky to have a radio. It sat in one corner with the chairs facing the radio as we listened to our favourite programmes. We liked Jack Benny, Bob Hope, and The Lux Radio Theatre. My brothers especially liked The Lone Ranger.

Every Saturday night we listened to the hockey game. Dad was a life-long fan of the Montreal Canadiens so we all boosted them as well. Everything stopped when the World Series baseball games were broadcast. Teachers cancelled classes so students could listen to the games on the radio in their classrooms.

The walls throughout our house were made of V-joint lumber. Actually, it was flooring put on upside down so there were deep grooves every three or four inches apart. It was fashionable but very hard to keep clean. In the living room was a plate ledge around the room, just above eye level on which one could display ornaments or pictures. On ours was a picture called "Spring Morn". This picture was infamous in the 20's as it showed a scantily clad woman bathing herself while standing in a pool. Now such art would not receive a second glance.

The kitchen had a table placed under a west-facing window. Dad made a substantial wooden bench for the three boys. Dad sat at the end of the table; he always cut and put the meat on our plates. Mother sat at the corner next to him and added the vegetables. As soon as our parents served us, we began to eat. Every mealtime Dad would say, "I hope no one is ready for a second serving yet. I have not had my first helping."

On the adjoining wall was a wood stove set out from the wall with distance behind it through which a child could walk. We used a cupboard space, intended as a broom closet, as storage space for firewood. The washing machine stood in the opposite corner.

Off this wall was a pantry. In it, there were shelves on one wall and a sink with a cold-water tap on the other. There were bins for sugar and flour and a counter near the sink.

When we first bought the house there were two sheds in the backyard. The larger one closest to the house was a woodshed. Dad made us a swing between the two sheds. If I swung too high, I got an electric shock from the frayed wires connecting the sheds, so Dad moved the swing so it hung in the opening of the woodshed. On a rainy day, I could swing into dryness and out to rain on every push.

In our yard stood two enormous stumps left from the original first-growth logging in the area. One stump was high enough to support a board to make a teeter-totter. Loggers had cut the other stump off near the ground and it was gradually rotting. We spent many hours breaking off pieces of the decaying wood and watching the ants scurrying about carrying their eggs to safety.

A path led from the back door, past the sheds to the outhouse. Some called this "the palace" with the Queen's throne, but we called it the toilet. Dad dug a deep hole in the ground and built a small shed over the hole for privacy. Inside he built a wooden bench with a convenient hole. Mother stacked Eaton's catalogue or a pile of newspapers beside the hole. Although I could sit and read these papers, that was not their primary purpose. Nailed on the inside door of our privy was the end of a tomato crate with the grower's name, Ten Hop Yuen, in large red letters. If a member of our family ever uses a generic Chinese name, it is never Chang or Wong, but Ten Hop Yuen followed by peals of laughter. Somehow, Ten Hop is just the right name for the inside of an outhouse. In the summer, Mother poured a generous amount of chloride of lime down the toilet to cut down on odours and to discourage flies. She bought it in the grocery store in round green boxes the size of a cocoa tin. This lime was a big selling item, but not available now, I suspect.

Although we had screened doors and windows, flies were plentiful in the house in the summer. We always had fly coils in the kitchen. Consumers bought them in cardboard packages similar to film canisters. After I pulled off the cap, I slowly unwound a tape about an inch wide from within it. This tape, covered with a sticky, glue-like substance, attracted flies. Flies homed in to the coil, thumb-tacked to the ceiling. When the fly got too close, the goo trapped its feet. When flies completely covered the tape, mother burned it in the kitchen stove. We also

9

had a fly swatter. I tried to see how many flies I could get in one hit, but never exceeded the "Seven at One Blow" as told in the fairy tale of the same name. However, I did come close.

Saturday night was bath night. Mother filled a huge copper boiler with water and heated it on the wood stove. She then brought in gunnysacks from the shed and spread them on the floor beside the stove to soak up any spilled water. The square, galvanized washtub would be set on the sacks. We took turns having our baths starting with the cleanest and working down to the dirtiest. I always made sure I had the first bath! After bathing, I would get dry and put on my pyjamas while Mother added more hot water to the tub. Then the second child would have his turn and so on until each person had a bath and his hair washed. While Mother was bathing each of us, Dad combed our hair, and cut everyone's finger and toe nails. It was a very efficient system.

During the week, my parents had a different routine. While Mother did the dishes, Dad got us ready for bed. In turn, we stood on the kitchen table, our feet soaking in a basin of water and Dad washed us from the top down.

A favourite game when we were all in our pyjamas was to play hockey in the kitchen. We used kindling sticks for hockey sticks and a ball for the puck. We would try to shoot into the goal that was between the legs of the kitchen table. Eventually, as I remember, the game began as fun but later became more frantic. When several children were crying from the hits on goal and the high-sticking, Mother would come and end the fun. Well, perhaps it was more fun for some than others

Laundry was an enormous job. First, mother put the huge copper boiler on the stove and filled it with pails of water from the cold-water tap in the pantry. Then she wheeled the washing machine from its corner to the centre of the kitchen. After the water boiled, mother carried it from the stove and emptied it into the washing machine. With a sharp knife, mother peeled the hard bar of P&G soap, into the water. When the soap dissolved, she put the white clothes into the washing machine. The agitator, a central fin shaped device, moved the clothes around to wash them.

While this was going on, Mother placed a backless chair next to the machine, placed the square washtub on it, and filled the tub with cold rinse water. She added bluing to the rinse water to make the clothes appear whiter.

The grocery store sold Reckitt's bluing in a small block about the size of a golf ball. To use it, mother pulled the string holding the cheesecloth bluing bag back and forth through the water, until the water turned the desired deep blue colour. The remaining bluing sat on a dish to dry out, ready for the next wash. A package of bluing would last for many rinses.

Next, mother wrung the clothes through the wringer attached to the washing machine and into the rinse water. She needed to be careful to fold buttons and zippers into the centre of the clothes or the buttons would all pop off and the zippers would break. Often clothes would catch and begin to rewind around the wringer. Mother had to be careful not to catch her hand in the wringer as she tried to get it to rewind and extricate the clothes. After rinsing the clothes, mother wrung the clothes through the wringer once again

Finally, mother hung the clothes outside to dry on the clothesline. Many neighbours judged homemakers by how early their clothes were out on their line in the morning, how white her white clothes were, and how neatly and systematically the clothes were pinned to the line.

Mother repeated this procedure for each batch of clothes. Cotton blouses, shirts, and tablecloths were always starched. She heated a

11

pan of water containing cornstarch on the stove. After the final rinsing, mother soaked these garments in the starch mixture, wrung them out by hand, and hung them to dry. This technique ensured that cotton clothes were crisp. Mother washed all the woollen clothes by hand and laid them out flat on towels on the rack to dry. Machine washing shrank woollen clothes.

Finally, mother emptied all the dirty water. The washing machine had a spigot near the bottom. She placed a pail under this tap to catch the water, which she then carried to the sink. In the summer, mother emptied the water on the garden. Wash water was valuable for irrigation as no one had hoses or a sprinkler. To complete the daily routine, mother washed the floor with the last pail of wash water.

Mother dried the clothes inside for much of the year, as it is very wet in the Fraser Valley. For this purpose, Dad made a clothes rack to hang in the kitchen. Dad was not a carpenter, but what he made was strong. The rack began with a frame about 12 feet long and 6 feet wide constructed from 2x4 lumber. Holes drilled in these boards held six lines of heavy galvanised clothesline wire. Mother raised and lowered the rack with a pulley. The rack was heavy when empty, but massively heavy when draped with wet clothes. Mother was constantly taking off smaller dried items and opening up and unfolding heavy objects like sheets, as more space became available on the lines.

Mother did laundry every day. We had three sets of clothes: one we had on, one in the laundry and one in the drawer for the next day. Every day was also ironing day, as everything required ironing. There were no wash and wear clothes, no perma-press and no steam irons. Mother first dampened the clothes, and then rolled them in towels so the moisture could spread evenly through the material. Then mother unrolled the dampened clothes and ironed them. Because the garments were still damp, mother placed them once again on the rack to dry.

Care of the clothes for a large family took much of the day, but the preparation of meals was also time-consuming.

Mother kept the stove full of wood, removed the ashes each day and put them on the garden for fertilizer. To clean the surface of the stove, Mother used Jet brand stove cleaner, a paste like shoe polish that was applied with a rag to a warm stove. Then she used another clean rag to polish the stovetop until it shone.

To make toast we took out the oven rack, placed it on the stovetop and then toasted about a dozen slices at once. Sometimes mother made hard tack. She placed bread in a slow oven until it dried out and became brown and very brittle. For a special treat, mother sometimes soaked bread in bacon drippings and fried it in the bacon pan.

We were jealous of others who had bread and cookies from the store. We had to eat homemade bread, cakes, and cookies. Mother loved to bake and we always had desserts for supper and cookies or cakes in our lunches for school. Often on a rainy day, mother would say, "I think we should make fudge today." And we did.

We always had an enormous garden. Mother planted our lot, the size of two city lots, with berries, fruit trees and vegetables. Mother canned hundreds of jars of fruits, jams, pickles and vegetables. Every day she canned at least one product. In the winter, we had a quart of vegetables and a jar of fruit for almost every dinner.

Outside the house on the west side, there was a small door, which was the entrance to the cellar. In it dad built shelves to hold the year's supply of canned goods.

In the yard were a well and beside it, a deep pump house. In the summer, mother kept milk and butter in a pail at the bottom of the pump house. Because the hole was so deep, food kept as cold as it would in a modern refrigerator. At mealtime, one of the children brought the pail up with a rope tied to the pail handle. No homes had freezers or refrigerators. Mother covered food stored in the pantry cupboard with a clean cloth or with waxed paper. Plastic and aluminium foil were not yet invented. In the summer, mother purchased meat in small quantities every day as we had no means at home of keeping meat or leftovers safely.

I learned to read before I went to school. It was my responsibility to read the funnies to my siblings each night. How I loved the smell of the printer's ink as I opened the paper! We sat on the floor in a row behind the kitchen stove. It was warm and cozy and, we thought, somewhat private. One day the comics had several symbols, # @& and so on, that I could not decipher. Mother explained that these meant swear words. Now I knew what to do. I re-read the comic strip replacing each symbol with every swear word I had ever heard (and they were many). My parents were shocked. I have never used any of these words since.

After we went to bed, the older children used to "Go on with the Ranch." We produced an ongoing western radio-drama in which we would follow the adventures of our three heroes for months on end. Ian was Bill, I was Betty and Donald was Buck. These were not imaginary friends: these were real people.

Our sister, Ruth Diane, was born on September 14th, 1936. I remember Mother bringing Ruth home from the hospital. She was a very small and sickly baby. We know now about the Rh factor but that was unknown in 1936. Later, doctors called these babies "Blue Babies". Mother put the crib next to the stove to be sure the baby was warm. She stoked the fire night and day. Ruth just lay there, still. She did not cry nor demand attention of any kind. People told Mother not to bother with this baby because she would not live anyway, but Mother did everything possible to keep her alive. Eventually, Ruth began to recover and to thrive.

The McDonald family was now complete, three boys and two girls. Dad, who loved to play poker, always said, "Now I have a full house. It is pretty hard to beat that."

Donald, Ruth, Joyce, Michael, Ian

Playtime

The games we played followed the seasons. In early spring, we played several different games with marbles. In the most popular variation, a ring was drawn with a stick on the ground and each person would place a marble in the ring. The purpose of the game was to shoot the marble out of the ring. The player held the marble between the bent right thumb and the index finger. Then, using the power of his thumb the shooter would try to hit one of his opponent's marbles. If he could hit the marble out of the circle, he kept the other person's marble. This was called "playing for keeps." Sometimes, if playing with a friend or a small child, he played just for fun, but that was not much of a challenge. Ian was the best shot in our neighbourhood and always had a tobacco tin full of his booty. Large marbles, called Cobs, were much prized, as were Steelies (ball bearings whose weight made them deadly). Sometimes a player could also sell his winnings if the opponent had "lost all of his marbles".

Boys also played "Cut the Pie". A large circle was drawn in compacted dirt or on the gravel road. An open pocketknife was thrown into the circle with enough force to cut into the dirt and remain standing upright. Wherever the knife stood, a line divided the circle (the pie) and the thrower would claim the largest piece. Then the opponent would hurl his knife and see if he could take over the biggest portion. The winner was the one who could continue to cut the pie so accurately that the other was left with virtually no pie at all. It reminds me of how Europe was divided after World War I. Perhaps that is how the game originated?

It was a common sight to see dozens of these games going on in the playground at the same time. Nearly every boy had a knife and no one would suggest it was inappropriate to play with knives at school. I never heard of anyone using a knife dangerously.

Marble season for boys was skipping season for the girls. The playgrounds were not divided, but the girls and boys did not play together at school.

A favourite game was played with a long rope, with a turner at each end. A skipper would run into the turning rope whenever the rhyme began, do the actions the chant suggested, and then run out when it ended.

A typical skipping rhyme:
> Teddy Bear, Teddy Bear, Turn around.
> Teddy Bear, Teddy Bear, Touch the ground.
> Teddy Bear, Teddy Bear, Go up stairs.
> Teddy Bear, Teddy Bear. Say your prayers.
> Teddy bear, Teddy Bear, Turn out the light.
> Teddy Bear, Teddy Bear, Say good night.

Then the skipper would wave, say good night and run out safely.

Other rhymes had counting features:
> I had a skinny sister who went to take a bath.
> She slid down the drainpipe
> And did we ever laugh.
> How many miles did she go?

One, two, three, and continue to count the number of jumps until the skipper either tripped on the rope or was too exhausted to continue. If the skipper missed and caught the rope on her legs, she had to exchange places with the girl at the end of the rope and the game continued.

To make the game more challenging, sometimes two long ropes were turned simultaneously in a game called Double Dutch. The ultimate challenge was to skip "Pepper" or even "Red Hot Pepper" which meant the ropes were turned as fast as possible. This was a way to trip up the best skippers, forcing them to take a turn on the ends of the ropes and giving other players a chance for a turn. If there were too few girls to play as a group, you could skip alone or double with a friend using a short rope. I liked to skip all the way to school, a distance of about a mile, by running as I turned my rope.

Following skipping season was hopscotch season. Adjoining squares were drawn with a stick on the road. A piece of broken glass was used as a marker. It was thrown into a square in a precise order, being sure the glass did not touch any lines and that it fell into the correct square. I then hopped from square to square, not touching any lines with my foot, picked up the glass while balanced on one foot, and returned to the starting line. If I were successful, I had a second turn and aimed for the next square in sequence. If not successful, my opponent had a turn. We had to repeat the same squares every turn until we were able to do it. The winner was the first to complete every square.

Later the girls played "O'Leary". This game involved counting and actions all done in time to the bouncing of a lacrosse ball.

The patter was:
One, two, three O'Leary
Four, five, six, O'Leary
Seven, eight, nine, O'Leary
Ten, O'Leary, One, two.

Each time I said a number, I had to bounce the ball, but when I said O'Leary, I had to do a particular action. Some actions were bouncing the ball high or low, spinning around, or bouncing the ball through my skirt which was held in my opposite hand. The climax of the game was doing all 15 O'Leary actions in correct order, one after the other without any bounces in between. This game required a great deal of coordination, especially as we liked to play it while walking to school. The sidewalk was not perfectly level so often the ball would roll onto the road or into the bushes at the side of the road. Once, my ball went into the deep ravine that housed the pump for the Abbotsford water system. I somehow managed to navigate a ragged trail through the bushes down to the water's edge by pulling myself by small branches and roots. I would never have given up retrieving my ball.

Another game, which developed eye-hand coordination, was "Jacks". For 10 cents, I got a small cotton bag, tied with a string, containing eight metal jacks and a small ball. I rolled all the jacks out on the floor. Then I bounced the ball, picked up one jack with the other hand and caught the ball before it hit the floor. After I succeeded in picking up all the jacks one at a time, then I tried to pick them up two at a time and so on until finally I picked up all eight jacks in one hand on one bounce. This is not easy with the small hands of an elementary school child

On summer evenings, all the neighbourhood children gathered in a field behind our house to play softball. We usually had enough players for two teams, but sometimes we had to play scrub. My brothers were by far the best players. In the early evening, all the small children and the girls would go up to bat first, but soon they were put out, and my brothers and the other boys were up for the rest of the evening, as all the rest of us ran aimlessly around the outfield and the boys made home run after home run.

Another favourite game was "Auntie-I-Over". We would divide into two teams, each standing on opposite sides of the house. Someone would yell, "Auntie-I-over" as a ball was thrown over the roof of the house. On hearing this, everyone would run to the other side of the house while the team, which had thrown the ball, would try to run and catch the other players before they reached safety on the other side. If caught, that person had to join the other team. The game was over when one team had all the players.

Michael at bat, Ian catching

A highlight of summer fun was when the bats came out. We would all get sticks and jackets and run about screaming and throwing our coats at the varmints. I wonder why we never caught one of them. We had a similar attack strategy for the swarms of flying ants that had their season, too.

When it began to get dark, we would usually play "Hide and Seek". Sometimes we would play "Kick the Can." This was a variation of "Hide and Seek" where a squashed can was put in the middle of a circle. It was kicked out as a signal to run and hide. Many evenings, following this game, Benny Biro, a neighbour about our age, would get out his accordion and play by the hour as we sang.

We had other adventures catching birds. Mother told us we could catch birds by putting a little salt on their tails. She wrapped a bit of salt in waxed paper and we would take it in hand, creeping cautiously after the birds and trying to get close enough to capture them. No matter how hard we tried, we never did achieve success. Now I realize how successful Mother was in keeping us busy outside for hours. Strangely, we fell for this ruse on more than one occasion.

One year we all made stilts from 2x4's. They were too heavy to move around quickly, but fun to make. We also made a variation by crushing tin cans to fit our feet and walking around on them.

All my brothers had paper routes and earned money to buy bicycles. I never had a bike nor learned how to ride. We all had roller skates and I spent hours on an abandoned tennis court. Skates were different from roller blades as they had metal clamps, which screwed the skates to your shoes. We gave no thought to the way these clamps tore the soles off our shoes. We took some severe falls, and badly scraped our knees, but no one wore protective clothing or a helmet. With the exception of softball gloves, no protective gear was available.

When the chestnuts fell in the late autumn, we played "Conkers". A hole was drilled through a chestnut and a long string was tied through it. A player held his conker firmly by the string. Then the other player would attempt to swing his conker and hit the opponent's with such force that the conker would be broken to bits. The winner was the one who broke the other's conker without damaging his own. A hardened conker was considered a treasure as it could break many conkers without being destroyed. There were deep discussions about the best way to select, and to drill the hole in the chestnuts. Of course, my brothers were the experts in my family.

Although I had several dolls, I took no great interest in them. However, I loved to play with paper dolls. My favourites were a set of the Dionne quintuplets. These paper dolls were a premium from Palmolive soap and much treasured.

The Quints, Yvonne, Marie, Annette, Cecile and Emily, were born near Callander, Ontario. The provincial government believed the Dionne parents were incapable of raising the babies and declared them wards of the province. The children lived by themselves with teachers and nurses in "Quintland", a home across the way from their parent's house. They seldom had contact with their siblings or parents. At appointed times the children, all dressed alike, were brought out into a fenced play area to be viewed by tourists and the media. Cars lined up for miles to see the children. My Aunt Joyce was one who traveled to see them.

When we were quite small, we spent a lot of time leaning over our back fence watching to see if any cars went past on what is now the Trans Canada Highway. Sometimes we would see two or three in an afternoon. A huge cloud of dust would surround the car and announce its arrival before we could see it clearly. The highway was paved shortly before World War II. It was exciting to see the paving project, but it was not so much fun to watch for cars without the beacon of dust to proclaim their imminent arrival.

Our family always played cards. Mother and Dad were excellent Bridge players. When I was about 12 years old, they told me I should learn to play, too.

"Play Bridge and you will always be able to make friends in a new community," they said.

We had a friend, Jack Mahoney, who had been a high rigger when Abbotsford was first logged off. He became my permanent partner. Every Sunday night for many years, he and I played Bridge against Mother and Dad. We kept a running total of our score for the year. The losing team always bought the winners a bottle of liquor for Christmas. As neither mother nor I drank alcohol, and Jack and I never won, in reality, Jack gave my dad a bottle every Christmas.

I learned to play badminton while in Grade Eight and it became another passion. In Grade 12 I played in the High School Provincial Tournament and later played for the Normal School team.

Provincial Badminton Team
Pat Clarke, Audrey Gleeson, Bill
Wallace (my partner)
Mr. Farenholtz – Coach

During school time, the family always spent the evening sitting around the big oak table in the living room. Mother would help us all with our homework or we would read together. We were taught to knit and embroider as we sat around that table. Ian knit many heavy wool socks. He would knit to the heel, then mother would turn it and Ian would knit to the toe before mother finished it off. Of course, we did not tell anyone outside our family that the boys could knit. They did have their reputations to uphold. I still have an embroidered dresser set that Michael made as a small child. We did not know then, that he was colour blind, so the selection of colours was rather unusual.

From the time we were very small, Mother always read to us. I am sure this explains why we are all now, as adults, such voracious readers. There was a small library in Abbotsford, located in what had once been a private home. Mother went to the library every week and always picked up two or three books. She could talk knowledgeably on almost any topic.

I also went to the library almost daily in the summer as we could take out two books at a time and it did not take long to read a primary book. One of the greatest thrills of my life was the day when the librarian told me, after I had read every book in the children's section, that I could go to the other side of the room and get a grown-up book: that is, one without pictures. Mother did not have to worry about the language or material in the books as writers were censored to keep literature suitable for even a pre-teen to read.

Pets We Loved

The first pet I remember was a beautiful collie dog, which Dad named Flossie after a teacher with whom he worked. One day we did not have her any more. My parents probably knew what happened to her, but for us children, she just "disappeared".

Donald with Flossie

Shortly after, Mother went downtown shopping and another collie followed her home and adopted our family. Mother later discovered that the dog had belonged to a farmer who had abused him. "Peter" was a great family friend for many years. As Ruth was about two years old at the time, Peter followed the instincts natural to the collie breed, and herded her whenever she was out in the yard. If Ruth would attempt to go near the road, he would gently nuzzle her back into a safe area to play.

Ian wrestling with Peter

Later, after I had left home, the family had a Beagle called Poindexter. He had the unique personality suggested by his name.

We also always had a cat. Of the series of cats, I remember particularly Jeffrey and much later, after I had left home, Ho Chi Minh. Ho Chi was partly a Siamese cat and was, therefore, nocturnal. One night when I was visiting at Mother's I woke with a start as Ho Chi leapt in the dark onto my bed, and right down the top of my nightgown. I let out a blood-curdling scream

23

destined to wake the whole family. My family thought it was clever of Ho Chi to pounce at night, but I never left the door open again.

Ian & Joyce with well loved cat

When my children were teen-agers, I saw a pocket book in the store called, "Ho Chi Minh's Lovers". I wrapped it for them to give to their Grandma for Christmas.

A few days after Christmas, Mother asked me, "Did you read the book before you sent it?"

"No," I replied.

Then after a long pause she asked," Did the children read it?"

"No, they wanted to, but I was anxious to put it in the mail," I answered.

"Well, thank heavens," Mother said. "That was the dirtiest book I have ever read. I burned it in the woodstove so there would be no chance of anyone else ever reading that book."

You might note that Mother read it, though.

One day my dad accidentally ran over Ho Chi. His head was badly crushed and it seemed as if he could not survive. A family friend, Trevor Clarkson, was a veterinarian and knew how precious the cat was to my mother. He wired Ho Chi's jaw in place. Eventually the cat recovered, and was always a much-pampered pet. He would eat only the most expensive tins of cat food and special morsels exactly to his liking. He really ruled the house as only a cat could do.

For several years, we had bantam chickens and on one occasion a large rooster we called Cicero. He was not exactly an orator, but he could get us all up at dawn. At about the time Cicero was the right size to kill, Auntie Jane came to visit us from Kisbey. It would be a treat to have roasted chicken. But no one would kill him.

"Well, this is so silly," said Auntie. "I will kill him." And she did.

But who would cook him? "Not I," said my mother.

"Well, you're being very silly," said Auntie. "I will cook him" And she did.

"Now, who would like a nice slice of chicken?" said my dad as he served our supper.

No one but Auntie ate any of Cicero. We never had another chicken as a pet.

Our neighbours across the street, the Gilmours, had two cows that they milked in the early morning and again at suppertime. We children liked to visit and watch the milking. I had a special interest in these cows as one was named Bessie, a typical name for a cow, but also my mother's name. The other was called Joyce. I believe this was my only namesake.

The farm cats would stand beside the cows waiting for a squirt of milk from the cow's udder. We would open our mouths, too, to get a taste of the warm, fresh milk. Usually, the milk would miss our mouths and run down the front of our clothes.

Donald, Michael & Poindexter

Health and Medical Care

We did not need a medicine chest in our house to contain the tin of Aspirin tablets and bottle of Vick's Vapour Rub, which comprised our complete store of medical supplies. If one of us had a cold or cough, he was liberally rubbed with Vick's and a wool sock was pinned around his neck to increase the effectiveness of the rub. Soon the patient was sweating and the cough seemed to improve. A hot drink with sugar and lemon juice also helped to stop a persistent cough.

If we had an infection, such as a boil or carbuncle (a staph infection, which resulted in a huge boil with several heads). Mother would chew bread, add brown sugar, apply this under a bandage to the infection, and leave it in place for a few days. Eventually, the infection would be drawn out and the sore healed. Penicillin was not discovered until some time during the Second World War when it was found in mouldy bread. The simple folk medicine of a bread poultice must have, unknown to us, contained penicillin. Other poultices included mustard plasters for congestion in the chest and onion poultices or soap poultices for infections.

Patients never went to the doctor. If someone was very ill, the doctor came to visit the patient at home. There was no medical insurance so the doctor was never called unless you were very ill. I cannot remember the doctor ever coming to our house.

Many illnesses that are routinely treated now were virtual death sentences. Tuberculosis was particularly dreaded. The only treatment that had any chance of success was to move the patient to a special hospital for TB patients, called a sanatorium. There was a large sanatorium in Tranquille, near Kamloops, another on Vancouver Island near Cobble Hill, and one for Natives near Chilliwack. Here, patients lay in bed, enjoyed fresh air and sunshine, and for most of them, waited to die.

27

It was considered shameful to have cancer. The word was not spoken. The newspaper obituary might use a euphemism like "died a lingering death" and the reader would understand that the person had died of cancer.

Because most milk was not yet pasteurized, undulant fever was common. There was no treatment.

Small pox was a dreaded disease that was often fatal and left those who survived with severe pocking of the skin. A vaccination was developed which prevented small pox and we all received this treatment when we went to school. I have seen many adults whose faces were seriously disfigured by small pox scars.

It was also common to see people with huge enlargements of their thyroid glands, which were called goitres. The soil in the Fraser valley is deficient in iodine, which lack causes this deformity. Before salt was routinely iodized in its preparation for market, this condition was rampant. To counter this, all children were given an iodine tablet at school each morning.

There were no inoculations for the other childhood diseases, such as measles, mumps, chicken pox or scarlet fever. Each winter there was an epidemic of one or all of these diseases. As soon as someone was identified as having one of these illness, a member of the Public Health Department would come and hammer a quarantine notice on the front door. That meant that no one could leave or enter your house for two weeks. With several children in a family, the quarantine could extend more than two weeks if not all the children contracted the disease at the same time. It was not known that the diseases were contagious in the days before the spots or rashes were evident so the quarantines were likely of little value. One winter our family had all three diseases; measles, mumps, and chicken pox, consecutively. We spent almost all winter in quarantine. My next door friend, Audrey, and I would play catch over the fence between our yards. So much for disease prevention!

In the early summer following this time, I became very sick with a high fever. I could barely walk. I remember crawling on my hands and knees to sit in the sun on the back porch. Later, when we heard about polio, my mother decided that is what I must have had. Fortunately, it was a mild case, if that was, indeed, what it was. I did not see a doctor.

None of the common products we can buy today in a modern drug store were available. There was no Kleenex. We used a cloth handkerchief. It was soaked in salt water to remove the mucous before being washed with the other clothes. We used a bar of soap to wash our hair and there were no conditioners, gels or sprays to hold hair in place. Men used Brylcream to smooth down their hair or, if they were hunters, they often used bear grease.

Donald, Ian petting the sheep, Bob Masson

There were no deodorants for sale, but there was Lifebuoy soap, which advertised that it stopped BO (body odour).

People in my childhood, would have been shocked to see advertisements for sanitary supplies and contraceptives. In the drug store, sanitary supplies were pre-wrapped in brown paper and placed out of sight. If a woman wanted to purchase such a product, she would have to ask a clerk to get it from the "secret hiding place" under the counter. In our home, we used the gauze covering on sanitary napkins as sterile bandages if anyone was cut. I thought that was their purpose and no one told me anything different for many years. It was against the law to sell contraceptives.

Clothing

For school, girls wore pleated wool skirts, and white starched blouses topped with a hand knitted sweater or cardigan. We also wore knee-length stockings and leather Oxfords. When it rained, we wore rubber galoshes, with metal clasps, over our shoes. We also had hand-knitted mitts and toques.

When I started school, I had a fur coat, which Grandma Pridmore cut down for me. It was great fun to pretend I was a bear, run after, and attack other children.

One winter Grandma sent me knitted over-pants. It was what girls wore on the prairies, but unknown in B.C. What was memorable about them was their colour: bright orange with wide black elastic around the waist. It was so embarrassing! I would sneak into the cloakroom to remove them before any of my classmates got a view of those monstrosities.

In summer, girls wore cotton dresses, often sleeveless and always with a slip underneath so they would not "show through".

Girls never wore shorts or slacks. Shorts became fashionable when I was about 10 years old and I begged for a pair. But dad used his favourite expression: "No daughter of mine will wear shorts."

It extended to such remarks as, "No daughter of mine will ride on a truck in a bathing suit," when I was asked to run for local Princess on May Day. And "No daughter of mine will walk downtown in the evening alone," even if it was still light.

I could go, however, if my brothers would walk several steps ahead and I would pretend I did not know them. They were also pretending they did not know me.

Joyce – age 12, 1942

However, dad was forced to allow me to wear shorts when the school requested students wear them for PE when I was in grade 8. Previously, girls could either do only those activities in PE, which allowed them to be lady-like or be immodest. No wonder a popular chant from the boys was:

I see London
I see France
I see *(fill an embarrassed girl's name)* underpants.

Even when I began to teach PE, in 1949, I wore white shorts, but had to cover them with a short white pleated skirt.

When young, my brothers dressed like English schoolboys. They wore short pants, white shirts, sweaters and Eton caps. Knee length socks and leather boots completed their outfits. Their boots had steel plates called blakies secured to the heels and toes to make them wear longer.

Grandma Pridmore, who had apprenticed as a dressmaker in England before her marriage, made us many clothes. When parcels arrived there was always something new for each of us. She remade Grandpa's pants into beautifully tailored, lined pants for the boys. In later years, the boys wore long overalls.

Nothing was wasted. Adult coats, dresses and trousers were unpicked, and washed. The pattern for the new garment was then applied to the reverse side of the fabric, cut out, and sewed.

Men's collars and cuffs were unpicked and turned to the good side and sewed on again. Buttons and zippers were unpicked and saved to mend other garments. Scraps of cloth became rugs and quilts. Finally, rags were used to wash the dishes or the floor.

Often mother would cut the feet off worn wool stockings, pick up the stitches and reknit new feet on the socks. Old woollen garments were saved and sent to a mill on the prairies that would exchange so many pounds of worn wool for gray blankets.

Donald in his favourite aviator hat
1938 - Arcola SK

Grandmother McDonald had a Singer sewing machine. Grandma did not sew, so mother received this machine. When a sewer wanted to use it, she pressed a button and the machine rose pneumatically into place from within its cabinet. It was operated by foot power on a treadle. I learned to control the speed and rhythm of the operation, by developing the correct speed to pump with my feet.

My mother did not enjoy sewing, though she did make many clothes and did the never-ending mending. I, however, took great pleasure in sewing and made almost all my own clothes in my teen years. When I married, Mother gave me this sewing machine and I used it for many years before buying an electric machine. I continued to remake my children's clothes from old garments just as I had learned from my grandmother.

Joyce, Audrey Gleeson
shopping
1947 - Vancouver

School Days in Abbotsford 1936-1948

What excitement when the first day of school arrived! It poured with rain on that eventful day. I set off with my lunch in hand accompanied by my dad who taught Grade 7 at the Abbotsford Elementary School. Gordon Gleeson, our next door neighbour and father of my best friend, Audrey, owned a business butchering meat and delivering it to various customers. He stopped and picked us up for school. He and Dad rode in the front of the truck. Audrey and I rode in the back with the meat. I wonder what the food inspectors would do now.

Later, I helped the janitor, Tom Andrews, sweep the schoolroom. I had certain "privileges" as the daughter of a teacher. Another privilege was to eat my lunch in the furnace room with my dad and the janitor. I think Dad ate there so he could smoke on his lunch break.

The school had a full basement where we played on rainy days. There were benches along one wall so students could sit if they did not want to run about. Usually the Grade Eight girls, who considered themselves too mature to play childish games, occupied these benches. Large pillars became bases for playing "Cat-in-the-Corner". Returning several years after leaving this school I was amazed to discover the basement was dark, dusty and dreary, and barely above my head in height. I remembered it as a paradise.

Off the basement were the bathrooms. Most children had never seen flush toilets, so on the first day of school we were taken into the basement as a class and taught how to flush.

After a teacher rang a hand bell to announce it was time to go into the school, the students lined up by two's. Grade 1 girls first, followed by Grade 1 boys, and then grade two's in the same way until everyone was in line. Absolute silence was expected as we waited to go inside. When everyone was quiet, we marched to the classroom like little soldiers.

A good teacher was one who kept the classroom absolutely quiet. If you wanted to answer a teacher's question, you stood straight beside your desk and replied, then sat down. Speaking out was strictly forbidden. When the principal came to the door, on the command the whole class would arise in unison and say, "Good morning, Miss Stenerson." Then on the command, "You may be seated now." we would simultaneously sit down.

Corporal punishment was common, not only in the home but also in the classroom. The motto "Spare the rod and spoil the child" was a by-word. We were always told if we were punished at school for bad behaviour, we would get twice the punishment when we got home. This was true in most homes. Good behaviour was highly prized. In general, children were to be "seen and not heard."

My parents never hit me, but I was a very meek and pliant child. My dad believed that one should not hit girls, but boys needed to be kept in line by stern means. One word from our father and we acted. I could not even imagine talking back to my parents.

Every classroom had a leather strap and a Bible in the teacher's desk. In the morning, the teacher read a prescribed section from the Bible, and then we recited the Lord's Prayer in unison.

After this, we had health inspection. The teacher walked down each aisle, looked at our hands and nails, saw whether we had clean faces and combed hair. If anyone was not clean enough to pass inspection, he was sent to the basement to wash. Then we each received an iodine pill and were ready to begin the day's work.

The strap was a constant reminder and threat to keep unruly students on task. It was enough. Often the teacher would dramatically take out the strap, slap it on the desk, and remind us to get back to work. This would quickly restore quiet. Some teachers were sadistic in the use of the strap. One I remember

36

gave a hit on the hand for every spelling mistake a student made on the weekly test. The ultimate punishment was to be sent to the principal's office to be strapped. You could hear the hit of the strap throughout the whole school. We would cower in our desks counting each time the strap hit.

"One, two ...nine, ten."

Then the culprit would swagger back to class.

"Didn't hurt. That teacher couldn't make me cry," he would brag, rubbing his sore hands on his pant legs.

The classrooms each had a cloakroom adjoining them in which each student had a hook for his coat. Above the row of hooks was a shelf for the lunches. We ate our lunches sitting at our desks with the teacher supervising our behaviour. I always had a sandwich, cookies and a fruit followed by a drink of water from the basement fountain. No one was allowed to remain in the classroom after eating. Few students went home for lunch as most lived at some distance from the school.

Within the classroom, all was in order. Desks, which were joined on wooden runners, were lined up in precise rows. To keep dust down, the floors were oiled several times a year. This oil ate away the soles of our shoes and had a very pungent smell when first applied.

In the top right hand corner of the desk was a round hole, called a well, to hold an inkbottle. We used a wooden penholder. In this, we slipped a metal nib with a slit in its point. The pen was dipped into the inkwell. Enough ink was held by the pen nib to write a few words. After each group of words, I used a blotter to absorb the excess ink. Then the process was repeated for the next few words and so on.

One student had the responsibility to keep the individual inkwells filled. The teacher mixed ink powder with water and filled a large bottle. You can only imagine the messes as small children tried to fill these little bottles. Our clothes often had ink stains and these stains did not wash out. In Grade Three, a student "got ink". As expected, the neatest writers first had the honour and privilege of

writing with ink, and then others would gradually be added to the list of those who were issued pens. Our books and clothes were covered in ink as we tried to master the amount of ink our pens would hold.

Joyce
Hand knitted dress & coat
made by Grandma Pridmore

Great effort was made to have our classrooms decorated for special seasons. Windows were covered with curtains made of crepe paper. Holly, maple leaves, or farm animals, cut from construction paper, were pasted on the windows to augment the units of study.

My Grade 1 teacher was Miss McLeod. I believed she was perfect. Everything she said was true and she knew everything. She became the ultimate authority. My parents grew weary of, "Miss McLeod says..."

Children did not pass to the next grade unless the prescribed work was mastered. In our class was a girl called Nellie who was about twelve years old. Audrey and I loved Nellie. As she could not read, I was often asked to help Nellie when I finished my work quickly. As I could read before I went to school, I had lots of time to "help Nellie". I do not know what became of her, but several years later she was still in grade one. Mother and Mrs. Gleeson, Audrey's mother, worried that Nellie might teach us things we should not know at our age, but they did not need to worry. Nothing Nellie knew could adversely influence us.

Miss Hunt taught Grade 2. She read us "Winnie the Pooh" which had been recently published. Each day we heard one more of Pooh's adventures. It is still one of my favourite books.

As a class project, we made chairs from orange crates. Oranges came in wooden boxes, divided in the centre by a thick wooden partition. One end was removed, then the sides were sanded and

38

later the chairs were painted a dark green. We used these chairs for our reading groups.

We had three reading groups, as did most classrooms. The bluebirds were the top group, followed by the robins who read at average level, then the squirrels that you know are on the ground. We were not supposed to realize that levels of achievement divided the groups but we all did.

I loved my Grade Three teacher, Miss Nye. Abbotsford School was overcrowded so the Grade Three class was moved to the Masonic Lodge building on the opposite side of the playground. We had an enormous classroom. A highlight of this year was the construction of an Eskimo village. At the back of the classroom was a large sand table. Our teacher bought a cut out set of a model Eskimo village, complete with several igloos, and many hunters and animals. After we finished our work, we were allowed to cut out, assemble and arrange the figures in this village. I think I did more than my share of the village. Later, I realized that the "squirrels" never had the opportunity to do the fun projects at school.

Our Grade 4 teacher was the music teacher for the school. I only remember her name. Why she wrote it out in full, Mabel B. Hind, I could never understand, as all the students found it hilariously funny.

The Grade 5 classroom was too crowded so a group of about six students was placed in Miss Baker's Grade Six classroom. We were disappointed, as we wanted to be in Miss McPhee's class. She was known to have fun with her students and we knew Miss Baker was very strict and no fun at all. It was our fate to have her for two years. At the end of two years, we completed Grade Five, Six and Seven. Then Miss Baker joined the army. After the war, she returned to the same school. The war made a change in her. Her students loved her. They said she was so much fun, and she was a competent teacher, besides. I guess the military teaches one to enjoy life!

Miss Stenersen, the principal, also taught the Grade 8 class. She was extremely strict, but fair. She had two obsessions. One was with grammar. We spent an inordinate amount of time parsing sentences. She had a complex system of brackets and squares for identifying clauses and phrases, nouns and verbs in every tense and mood. She drilled us mercilessly. I must admit it was useful in studying French in high school, but at the time, we saw no use for this exercise.

Her other obsession was with Sir Walter Scott's poem "The Lady of the Lake". We analyzed it almost word for word, phrase by phrase, for week after week. Worse, we had to memorize long sections, much of which I still can recite. The ability to memorize was considered very important and much of our learning was by rote.

Audrey Gleeson, Dorothy Mae McBeth, Joyce, Ruth Weins
Joanne Clement, Ruth Siemens
Grade 4 Mexican Project

In school, I liked to be in drama. In Grade four, I wrote a Halloween play, which was produced by my class. One year I played Alice in "Alice in Wonderland" In Grade 8, the school produced a musical, Foo Chang, with a Chinese theme. I played a secondary lead, one that did not require solo singing, you can be sure. Later, in High School, I took drama and acted in the play "Abraham Lincoln" in the Drama Festival.

Each year students entered the Fraser Valley Music Festival. Our class always sang in the choir and entered the dance section. One year we danced the Highland Fling and another year we did the Sailor's Hornpipe.

May 24th was called Victoria Day in honour of Queen Victoria. Abbotsford always had a special May Day event. One year I was a flower girl to the May Queen. Several years I danced in the May Pole dance, a tradition on May Day in England and thus also in the colonies.

Grandma McDonald played the piano for many community events, including school musicals and one year, a memorable fashion show. A textile manufacturer came to Abbotsford to promote its fabrics. I was asked to be a model. One of the outfits was an orange flowered sports outfit that consisted of shorts joined to a sleeveless top.

Dancing the May Pole

When I got about half way across the stage, I heard a great hiss from the woman in charge of the show. "She's got the thing on backwards."

"Well." I thought, "There's no way I'm going to turn around, go off the stage, change my outfit and come on again."

So grandma kept playing and I kept doing the prescribed walk and turns. I thought if I could not tell the front from the back of the outfit; neither would the audience.

There was no room in Abbotsford for our Grade Nine class so we were bussed to Sumas Prairie Elementary School where a boyhood friend of my dad's, Thomas Lindsey, taught us.

After completing Grade Nine, we returned to Philip Sheffield High School. The school had two entrances located on opposite sides of the school. One entrance was for girls and one for the boys. Our lockers were located near these outside doors, also. Grade 10 and 11 classes were separated so there were no boys in our classes.

By Grade 12, many students had left school to join the military, get married or go to work. Most of those left at school planned some kind of further education. For the first time in high school, we had co-ed classes. Most of our teachers were old (we thought) or women, as most able-bodied young men had joined the armed forces. Many teachers came out of retirement to do their share for the war effort. One of our French teachers must have been 80 years old and could barely walk.

There were very few electives. Typing and shorthand were offered, but academic students never took these courses. In Grade 12, I took Mathematics, English Literature, English Language, French, Chemistry, and History. As electives in high school, I took Home Economics and Drama.

There was no Senior Matriculation (Grade 13) offered in Abbotsford when I finished high school. Dad went to the Mennonite Institution in Clearbrook, and asked if I could enroll there. At first the principal told Dad that I could not enroll, as I would not fit into their religious classes. Later he phoned Dad and told him that they had investigated my record and I could attend there, but by this time Dad had another scheme. He contacted many parents from my Grade 12 class and was able, with other parent's support, to petition the School Board to have Grade 13 offered in Abbotsford. We had 13 students including one returned war veteran on his military credits. Because of the overcrowding following the war, we held some of our classes in a cloakroom.

Chemistry Lab, Phillip Sheffield High School

We all studied the same academic courses, taken in Grade 12, but I took Physics as well as Chemistry. I thought at that time, I would probably teach Mathematics as my interests tended to the sciences.

42

Philip Sheffield High School was accredited, which meant that if a student received a mark of at least C+ in a particular subject, he did not have to write the final exam in that subject. I never wrote a final exam in high school. In effect, this meant that I could relax at the end of the term, not worried about whether I would succeed in the government exams.

Mother & Joyce
Shopping for Graduation
1947 - Vancouver

A student did not take part in the Graduation Ceremony unless he actually graduated. It was not a recognition ceremony for mere attendance at school as many graduations have now become. In the afternoon of the last day of school, a ceremony was held in the school gym where each graduating student received a diploma.

Nothing ever changes. The principal, the School Board and other dignitaries gave us words of advice none of which I remember. I do remember my dress, however. All the girls wore white, short dresses and we had corsages, the first most of us had ever had. A tea for the mothers followed this event in the Home Economics room.

In the evening, we had a dinner prepared by our mothers, followed by a dance in the Anglican Church hall. Everyone was home by 11. There was no question of an all-night party, or liquor being served. Of course, it would not be.

For this occasion, I had my first evening dress. No stores in Abbotsford sold evening gowns, so mother took me to Vancouver on the bus to shop for an appropriate dress. Although it is only 45 miles to Vancouver from Abbotsford, I had only been there twice before and it was a thrill to go so far away to the city. My dress was pale pink with a lacy top that formed the sleeves as well. Little ribbons tied in bows decorated the front.

The only bursary offered to our graduation class was one for $100 offered by the Lion's Club. I was fortunate to be awarded this honour. It paid my full tuition to Normal School, in Vancouver the following year.

Mother & Joyce at High School
Graduation -- 1947

Special Occasions

The most eagerly awaited event was Christmas. Dad would take us out into the woods to chop down an appropriately sized fir tree.

Mother would shout after us, "Make sure it's not too tall."

Trees growing in the bush appear smaller than they do when standing in the living room. Dad always had to saw off several feet before dragging the tree into the house. As his father did before him, Dad took two huge nails and pounded the tree securely into the floor. Another nail was pounded into the wall behind the tree. Heavy galvanized wire was secured around the tree and to this nail. The tree never fell down!

Onto the tree, Dad strung a string of lights with eight coloured bulbs. Fragile glass ornaments and silver strings of glistening tinsel were added next. Finally, we children were each given a handful of icicles to place one by one on the tree. No tree was ever as beautiful as ours. We would sit by the hour admiring this tree with its shimmering beauty.

On Christmas Eve, we each hung up our stocking. These were not fancy decorated stockings as you see now, but one of our own stockings. As if by magic, on Christmas morning the stockings were filled. In the toe was a Mandarin orange, (we called them Jap oranges), then some nuts and special Christmas candies. Some were hard coloured candies in the shapes of ribbons and others a hard cream candy available only at Christmas time. We did not realize these were the same candies our parents had purchased. We knew they came from Santa Claus. We did not notice, either, that there might be fuzz from the wool sock caught on the sticky candies.

On Christmas morning, we had a special breakfast. First mother served grapefruit, a rare treat; followed by puffed wheat cereal. This was also a treat as we ordinarily had oatmeal for breakfast.

45

Then the greatest treat of all. We received our gifts from the tree. Nothing was placed under the tree until we went to bed so we had no idea what might await us. Usually we received needed clothes, but there were also toys and, best of all, sometimes a book. We always received gifts from our grandparents, uncles and aunts when we were young.

Looking around, Grandpa McDonald always said about the toys: "If they last half an hour, they'll last a year."

Some toys, then as now, were flimsy. Celluloid Cupie dolls and paper airplanes were fragile. One year my brothers received a tin copy of the Hindenburg and one of the China Clipper, famous planes of the day. They also had lead soldiers. Anything about aviation was new and exciting. My brothers had leather aviation hats to wear in the winter complete with earflaps and goggles. My brothers looked like little Charles Lindbergh's, the famous aviator.

All this excitement was followed by a turkey dinner. This was the feast of the year. The turkey was served with candied sweet potatoes, mashed potatoes and gravy, stuffing and peas. For dessert, we had Christmas pudding with hard sauce and mince meat pie.

When we became older, our Christmas routine changed. On Christmas Eve, all our relatives came to our house. This included Grandma and Grandpa McDonald, Aunt Elsie Webster and her family, Uncle Duncan and his family and other unmarried uncles. A few years my Grandma and Grandpa Pridmore were also there. First, we would open our gifts together. Then Mother would serve refreshments to everyone. Christmas fruitcake, mince tarts, fancy cookies and squares, and homemade candy were all enjoyed. It was so much fun to be together.

The McDonalds are all extroverts and storytellers. But my dad was the best storyteller of all. He would be in the spotlight most of the evening and everyone would be regaled by one joke after another. My brother, Ian, also has this gift. Then all the McDonalds went to Midnight Mass and the children went off to bed. We considered it a treat to be allowed to stay up so late as my parents insisted on early bed times on all other days.

The next best time of the year was my birthday. The countdown began long before the special day. It was not common to have birthday parties, but I did have one for my 10th birthday. I invited enough friends to fill the dining room table. I cannot remember what happened to my brothers and sister. They must have been sent to the kitchen.

 Mother always put money in the birthday cake. The money was sterilized, and then placed in convenient places in the cake so each child got a coin in his piece. The rule was, if you did not get a coin, you could have a second piece of cake. Later, when I had my own family, I continued this tradition. Strangely, Ted always got a 50 cent piece in his slice. I do not see why this was unusual for a man who could not only wiggle his ears, but also take a dime out of a child's ear or elbow.

We usually received clothes for our birthdays. Just before my 11th birthday, I saw in Eaton's catalogue the most beautiful pair of shoes I had ever seen in my life. They were patent leather and had a barrel shaped piece of wood stapled to the front as a decoration. We always wore sensible, leather oxfords with lace ties. These shoes had no ties but were glamourous, shiny, black, and to die for.

"No," said my Mother, "They won't last a week. That decoration will fall off in a day. You absolutely cannot have those shoes."

Can you imagine my utter joy when my birthday arrived and so did those shoes? Of course, my Mother was right. In a few days, the wooden barrels fell off and the patent leather cracked. In fact, if I were to be honest, the shoes were not even comfortable, but they remain the most memorable shoes I ever had.

Easter Dinner
Jack Mahoney, Mother, Uncle
Alex
Andy Devine, Dad

47

Another special day we looked forward to was Easter Sunday when we, for many years, had dinner with Jack Mahoney, my long-time bridge partner. Before retirement, his friend, George Taylor, had been a cook in the logging camp where Jack also worked. Each year they prepared a meal as George must have done for the camp. They always had turkey, ham and roast beef, heaping bowls of at least eight kinds of vegetables, and perhaps nine kinds of desserts. Instead of a tablecloth, Jack covered his table with sheets of newspapers. When food spilled on the paper, he would remove a layer of paper and leave the next layer exposed to do its duty.

Invited guests included our family of seven, Uncle Alex (Dad's bachelor uncle), and Andy Devine, a friend of Jack's who we always referred to as "The Sugar King" as he worked at Roger's Sugar Refinery in Vancouver. An onlooker would not notice the amount we ate despite the best efforts of my brothers.

Jack and Andy had grown up together in New Brunswick and regaled us with stories of fishing from a dory in the Atlantic. Most of the stories seemed to revolve around the expression,

"Hurry, Rory. Get the dory. There's an 'erring in the bay."

We never could figure out what this expression meant in relation to the stories.

Later George, who had a beautiful voice, would sing Irish songs, notably "Danny Boy", and Jack would join in the chorus.

Job Opportunities

The principal source of income in the Fraser Valley for teenagers was berry picking. The season began with strawberries in late May. Students were allowed to leave school early to pick berries, but my parents would not allow us to miss school. Later, raspberries ripened and often whole families, mothers and children together, went to the berry fields to work. Trucks came into town to pick up the workers, and deliver them to the outlying fields, and then returned them at night when the day's picking was over. I, however, walked about a mile to Freddie Verch's small plot on the Gladwin Road. He and his mother had only a few rows of berries which required just my family and a few more pickers for the harvest.

Like all pickers, I wore a "belly-buster", a tray holding two boxes of berries, tied around my waist. When these were filled I went to the flat, a large crate holding 12 boxes of fruit, which was cached at the end of the row in the shade, and exchanged the full boxes for empty ones and continued the process. Mrs. Verch trailed down the rows making sure no berries were missed and no branches were broken.

It was fun in the berry patch as we talked, told jokes and sang all day. We learned many things from other berry pickers that we could not tell our parents. Some migrant workers from the city were always lured to come out to the valley. They had the reputation of being very worldly, even immoral. I think Mother believed we were protected from their influence by going nearby to the Verch farm instead of travelling on the truck to outlying farms. We were not.

Girls also baby-sat, though it was called "looking after children". For an evening's work, I received 25 cents. I could not accept money from my aunts or anyone whom my parents invited to our home.

Boys had paper routes. There was a clear distinction between what boys could do and what was appropriate for girls. Naturally, boys had a great deal more freedom than did girls.

Most families believed that it was more important to educate boys than girls, as boys would have to support a family but girls would "just get married". Most opportunities not only for education but also for job advancement were reserved for men. I wished then that I had been born a boy.

My brothers sold cascara bark as another money raiser. Cascara trees grew profusely near Abbotsford. The bark was used medicinally as a laxative. The boys peeled the bark off the tree in strips and then carried it home in burlap sacks. The bark was spread out on the roof to dry thoroughly. If it threatened to rain, the bark was quickly picked up, brought into the house, and then set out again when the weather improved. When the bark was completely dry it became quite brittle. It was then broken into small pieces and sold by the pound.

Ian had a trap line on Matsqui Prairie Flats, a swampy bog traversed by streams, not far from our house. Ian brought home the animals he trapped, mostly muskrats, then turned the furs inside out and stretched them on wooden frames to dry. When a sufficient number were prepared he would sell them to a fur dealer.

 When I was 12, I got a permanent job at the Overwaitea grocery store. At that time, Overwaitea was principally a coffee and tea importer and blender. The store's original selling gimmick was to give the customer seventeen ounces of tea for each pound weighed, hence the name Overweight Tea shortened to Overwaitea.

During the war, many foods were rationed. Special coupons, coded by colour, were needed to buy sugar, tea, coffee, butter and meat at the grocery store. For example, sugar was allotted at half a pound per person per week, which is equivalent to a cup per week. I was hired to come to the store each day after school and glue these coupons on special forms to be sent to the government.

50

Many foods came to the store in bulk and I later advanced to weighing and packaging these foods. I scooped out white and brown sugar, tea, coffee, raisins, prunes, cocoanut and many other items from large barrels or boxes, poured the food into brown paper bags, and weighed it on a balance scale. I then sealed the bags with brown tape which I moistened with a damp cloth so the glue would stick. Finally, I wrote the name of the food and its weight on the bag with a grease pencil.

There were no plastic bags or Scotch tape. Under the counter were mounted large rolls of brown paper placed on metal holders each with a cutting edge to tear off a suitable piece of paper used to wrap the customer's groceries. The package was tied with string which the clerk broke off from a ball hanging from the ceiling. It was quite a knack to break the string in a special way by holding the string in your finger, giving it a twist, and allowing friction to cut the string. I felt very grown up when I learned to do this.

Customers did not touch the groceries on the shelves. They went up to the counter and told the clerk what they wanted. The clerk then took his pencil from behind his ear and wrote the items down in an order book. When the order was complete, the clerk walked around the store picking up all the items. Then the clerk, not on an adding machine, added the bill mentally. Sometimes the customer would pay cash, but more often, the customer charged his groceries until payday when he paid for the whole month's groceries. During the war mother kept her grocery bill under $30 a month for a family of five children. From this, she received a ten percent employee discount.

Usually a customer dealt with the one store where he had an account. Most customers never went to the opposition's store. This loyalty was very important during the war as scarce items were never put on the shelf but were set aside at the back with faithful customer's names on them. Such items as candy, cocoanut and raisins became rewards for a customer's trade. When a customer paid his bill at the end of the month, the manager would usually give him a dozen oranges or one of these prized scarce foods as a thank you for his business.

The price of food was controlled during the war so there were no changes in food prices until after the war ended. I knew the price, by memory, of every item in the store. The prices were written on the shelf, but not on the product so clerks needed to know all the prices by heart. I still remember many of those wartime prices. For example, a pound tin of Fry's cocoa cost $0.39.

Overwaitea Staff - 1948
Leonard Wallace, Ian McDonald, Joyce McDonald, Phil Swift
(Manager), Lorne Vanetta, Marg McLeod, George Cleal, Bill Kielo

Many customers preferred to phone in their orders. The clerk wrote the items in an order book. It became one of my responsibilities to fill these orders when I went to work after school. I would pick up the items (in my arms), pack them in boxes, add the bill, and place the boxes ready for the deliveryman to take to the customer's house. Grocery carts were a long way in the future. Usually the manager delivered these orders after work, but sometimes, if there were too many orders, a deliveryman was hired for this purpose. A customer was not charged to have his groceries delivered.

Later, I had the responsibility of checking the addition of the customers' bills each day and adding the monthly statements for each customer.

Twice a year we took inventory. When I was in senior high school, I was given the job of checking the inventory sheets. Once the stack was counted, I had to calculate the value of the stock. As most products came in cases of 24 and the costs were represented in fractions of a cent per item I really needed to be able to work with fractions in expanding these figures. The math was all done with a pencil and paper.

I worked for the Overwaitea for six years, eventually working as a clerk. I gradually received pay increases until I earned $.35 an hour. From these wages, I saved $750, which was enough money to go to Normal School for one year. This amount was equal to half a year's salary for a teacher at that time. Half a year's pay for a beginning teacher would now be about $18,000 dollars.

The War Years
1939-1945

I knew nothing about war until about 1937. At that time, movie theatres always showed a short news broadcast. The Spanish Civil War was in progress. The film I saw showed small children being strafed by low flying planes as they tried to run for safety into ditches along the road. I remember sobbing when I got home. I had nightmares from such brutality. I can still see this picture in my mind's eye.

In August 1939, I was visiting my grandparents in Greenwood, a small village in the Kootenays. The mailman came to the door and was talking to Grandma, who was a mother of eight sons.

"Well, Mrs. McDonald, I expect they will be taking all of your boys."

"But they won't take my dad," I interrupted.

"Oh yes," he said. "They will take everyone." The picture of small children scrambling to escape from low flying bombers returned to my mind.

At home, the threat of war increased. My family often sat in a semi-circle facing the radio as we listened to Adolph Hitler speaking at rallies in Germany. We did not understand what he was saying, but we could understand the threatening tone in the Fuhrer's voice and the thunderous applause of the German people as we imagined they raised their arms and heard the shout, "Heil Hitler."

Dad

My father, a school teacher with five children, was not required to enlist, but he did join the army as soon as he completed the school term. He told mother he wanted to go to Powell River to see a paper mill in operation. He returned a day earlier than mother expected and told her he had joined the Rocky Mountain Rangers. She was not surprised.

As Dad was an exceptional athlete and had taught Physical Education, he continued to teach the same courses in the army. Canada was not prepared for war after the Great Depression. Factories could not keep up with the sudden demand for uniforms. Dad instructed PE at the army camp in Vernon in the heat of the summer in the wool serge suit he had worn in the classroom. His platoon had one uniform at first. The soldier on leave wore this available uniform. It was irrelevant whether it fit perfectly as a soldier could not leave the Base in civilian clothes.

56

This situation did not last very long as the war effort increased and factories that had closed during the depression began to work furiously to fill the demands of the war. Almost everything for the domestic market was in short supply. The motto was," Use it up, make it do, or do without."

One day in 1942, I was again visiting my Grandma. A boy on a bicycle came to the door with a telegram. In the days before most people had telephones, this was always a dreaded sight. The messenger delivered a telegram that my uncle, James Edward McDonald, was missing in action and presumed dead. James was the rear gunner in a bomber on a raid over Essen, Germany. Artillery shots hit the plane, but it continued to fly until it crashed over Holland. For a year after James was killed, Grandma stopped playing the piano except for the song "Always" that she played over and over.

Grandpa and Grandma Pridmore visited for several months every winter while Dad was in the army. We had a large map of the world on our kitchen wall. It was an advertisement for Neilson chocolates and had large Crispie Crunch chocolate bars on each corner. (It is no wonder they are still one of my favourites.)

In the evening, Grandpa would talk about the daily battles and we would put markers on every battle site. Frequently the newspapers had full-page lists of military personnel wounded, missing or killed in action. Many were our friends or neighbours. When Dad was home on leave, I often saw him in tears as he read the names of his army buddies in the casualty lists.

One week Dad came home on embarkation leave. His unit was leaving for Italy. What a sad time as we realized we might never see our father again. Then a miracle occurred. When Dad returned to camp, his orders had been changed, a transfer to the Royal Canadian Engineers. Almost every man in Dad's unit was wounded or killed in the campaign up the Italian Boot.

James Edward McDonald

Although Dad did not go overseas, he did serve in the army for almost six years. When Dad returned home, I was in Grade 11. It was an adjustment for the family to have a father who was not a visitor. I do not think we realized until we were much older what a sacrifice both our parents made for the war effort.

All returning veterans were promised their former jobs when the war ended, but Dad did not want to return to his job as a school teacher. His war credits were approximately $750. This was about the same amount I had saved to go to Normal School. Dad suggested we pool our resources and buy a small confectionary store, possibly in Hope, BC, but I refused to do this as I had my heart set on teaching. Both parents advised me that teaching was a very difficult career for a woman and tried to persuade me to do something else, but I would not listen. Dad then set up a real estate and insurance business in Abbotsford with his brother, Don.

Rocky Mountain Rangers march from Kamloops to Vancouver
Dad's former students bike out to meet him
circa 1941

My parents subdivided their property and, with the money from the sale, made many changes to their home. Hot water was installed, and later a bathroom was added. A refrigerator and electric range made work easier. The house was jacked up and a basement was built under the house. An extra bedroom was added downstairs for the boys and the girls shared the bedroom upstairs. A wood burning furnace replaced the living room heater.

Best of all, though, Dad bought a car. There was a shortage of vehicles as all manufacturers had devoted their production lines to military vehicles during the war. Veterans had first chance to get new cars once the war ended. Dad got one of the first new cars after the war. It probably helped that Dad's brother, Duncan, and brother-in-law, Jimmy Webster, owned the local Ford garage.

On Sundays, we went for drives into the country just to explore unfamiliar sights. There was very little traffic especially on the back roads and logging trails that we liked to investigate. In the summer, we always carried pails to pick whatever wild berries we might find. On one occasion, we were picking berries on a logging road north of Harrison Lake. As we picked around a huge clump of berry bushes we were surprised to meet a large black bear walking around the same clump of berries in the opposite direction. I think the bear was as frightened as we were because he ran off immediately. Surely, he should have heard a large family talking and rattling their pails.

Another Sunday we were exploring again above Harrison Lake on a corduroy road. This type of road is made of small trees laid side by side, often to cover wet or uneven ground. Dad had a new car and this was its maiden trip. Somehow, the car slid off the road and hung with one wheel in the bush below the road. We were miles from help, cell phones were not yet invented, and no one would know where to look for us, if or when we were missed. Eventually Dad managed to use poles as levers, raised the car back onto the road and got us safely home.

On another Sunday drive, we went to what we called Blueberry Hill, on the Hope Princeton Highway, some distance east of Hope. It was near here that my Grandpa McDonald worked during the war. Japanese men, deported from the coast, were used to construct the highway. Grandpa was the foreman of one of these crews. The men lived in a camp by a river just below Blueberry Hill. We packed a lunch, took our pails and spent the day picking berries in our secret blueberry spot. Mother and Dad both smoked and on one occasion, Mother dropped some ashes from her cigarette onto the tinder dry brush. A fire started and we had a frantic time before we managed to get the fire completely out.

In later years, an earthquake occurred in this area and Blueberry Hill slid off the face of the mountain, rolled across the highway, and filled in the deep ravine to the river, completely covering all remains of the work camp.

Blueberry Hill
Mother, Dad, Michael, Ruth, Donald
circa 1947

Normal School
1948-1949

I was disappointed to go to Normal School. It was my dream to go to University to prepare to teach mathematics, but I had only enough money saved to study for one year.

"But," I rationalized, "I will go to Normal School, teach, and somehow save enough money to complete my degree."

Joyce 1948

Two weeks before school started, I took the train to Greenwood to visit my grandparents. Returning home, I was surprised to get a telegram on the train.

"Do not get off the train in Matsqui. Go directly to Vancouver. Your parents will meet you there." I could not imagine what serious emergency must have happened

When I arrived, my parents whisked me directly to the Normal School for a medical examination. You could not be accepted for teacher training unless you were medically fit. All the women were in one classroom where we undressed and were examined in a long line-up by a battery of doctors. The men had their exam in a separate room nearby. Perhaps the doctors should have given us some kind of psychological exam, too. I was very embarrassed to undress in front of others. Later, we had to gang shower after our PE classes. I never got used to that.

For the first few months at Normal School, I boarded with mother's cousin, Mary Charlesworth, who lived near 22nd street and Cambie. It was just a short walk as the school was across the street from City Hall at 10th and Cambie.

George, Mary's husband, was retiring from Spencer's Store and was building a house in Sidney on Vancouver Island. I had to find another place to stay. Mary knew a woman who sang in her church choir who would let me live at her house. It seemed like an ideal arrangement. The house was nearer to school at the corner of 16th and Oak and, although I did not know Mrs. Sulman, she was strongly recommended.

I shared the room with another student teacher, Barbara. We had two single beds and a four-drawer dresser that we shared. The closet had been removed and a stand was set in this space, which held a two burner electric hot plate. Near this was a shelf on which we kept our dishes, pans and food. Across the street was a corner store where we bought just enough food for each meal.

One weekend the Sulman's announced they would be away for a few days and asked me if I would like to use their oven to do some baking. Would I? What a question! The stove was a gas range, which needed to be lit with a match. I got everything ready, and then leaned over to light the gas. Suddenly there was a huge explosion. The oven door blew off; and the sides of the stove bulged outwards. Smoke and soot filled the room. Luckily, I was not hurt, but badly frightened. I cleaned the mess and paid for the stove to be repaired. I remember it cost $150, enough surely, to buy a new stove. I never again in my life used gas. I did not tell my parents about this crisis, as they would have worried about me.

The Sulman's were very different from any people I had ever met. Mr. Sulman worked in a bank. At 4 in the morning, we could hear the shower as he got ready for work. He always wore a suit so I presumed he was a bank manager, or at least a teller. In fact, he operated the lunchroom at the bank. At home, he wore trousers with a belt made of several neckties wrapped around his waist, and his undershirt. An extra supply of ties was wrapped around the doorknobs, so it took two hands to open a door.

One day when I came home, Barbara was very excited. She had looked out our bedroom window and seen Mr. Sulman on a platform in the yew tree near our window. He was stark naked. We never found out whether he was merely sun bathing or actually trying to peek in. We always kept our curtains closed after this and checked carefully to see if he might be able to see into our room.

Another day when I came home, I found Mr. and Mrs. Sulman wrestling in the kitchen. She had his shoulders pinned to the floor.

"She always beats me," Mr. Sulman complained. Not bad for a woman in her 60's.

As in high school, our classes at Normal School were divided into women's classes and men's classes. My class had all women whose last names began with L, M and Mc. Many of the men were older as they were war veterans going to school on their war benefits, but most of the women had come directly from high school.

There was a severe shortage of teachers in rural areas immediately after the war and some of the women in my class had taught in one-roomed schools for a year after completing Grade 12. Now they were back in school to get their diplomas. I had completed Grade 13, which was equivalent to first year university, so I had more education than did many others.

Mornings began with an assembly, arranged by each class in turn. We read the Bible, recited the Lord's Prayer, and then the assigned class put on a short programme. The purpose of the assembly was to give us ideas for the concerts and programmes that we would be in charge of when we went out into small communities. Most teachers expected to have Christmas concerts to arrange. Schools were usually the focus of the social life in rural areas and teachers were expected to plan and coordinate sports as well as cultural events.

Then we returned to our homeroom where the class attendance was taken. Each teacher in training had a classroom register as we would have the following year in our own classrooms. We would mark the attendance in the prescribed way, a / for morning attendance, a \ for afternoon attendance and a dot for tardiness. At the end of the month, we added the columns vertically and horizontally so the totals should balance. We were graded by how neatly and accurately we kept our registers, which we handed in to be marked. Registers are legal documents and are preserved indefinitely so must be kept accurately.

One day our teacher, Mr. Ozard, came in and said, "Miss McDonald, you are the only teacher who will get her pay on time this month." Mine was the only register which had balanced.

Later, when I taught in Langley, the School Board Office was next door to Langley Central Elementary, where I taught. At the end of the month, I would balance my register, and then take it next door to be checked before I got my pay cheque. You would have to stay at school as late as necessary to have it correct, because, indeed, your cheque was held up as long as it took to get the register balanced. The end of June was often a panic time for teachers who were mathematically challenged, because errors, which may have been compounded and carried over for months now, had to be resolved. How different it is now as classroom attendance is kept by a secretary on a computer.

In order to graduate from Normal School, a student had to prove competency in Mathematics and English to the Grade 8 level. In my naiveté, I supposed everyone at Normal School would have these skills. But it was not so. We wrote a test in these subjects upon reaching Normal School in September. If not successful, you tried again at Christmas, at Easter, and again in June. Failure to pass by this time meant the student had to withdraw.

Besides our marks on exams and assignments and on our practicums (practice teaching), a quarter of our final mark was based on what was termed our "personalities". I suppose that was a way to eliminate those whose marks were satisfactory, but who, for whatever reasons, were not deemed to be "teacher material".

To prepare us to be teachers we were expected to dress professionally. In fact, it meant that we must always wear silk stockings to school rather than the loafers and bobby socks we used to wear in high school. Also, we were never addressed by our first names. It took a while to realize I was Miss McDonald -- you know, the one with the silk stockings.

I became a part of a group of about eight students who did everything together. As I no longer had a job after school, I had time to do other things. We all played bridge and badminton. We spent a lot of time at the beach and often went dancing either in the Anglican Hall, which was a haven for young adults, or at the WK, a club in Chinatown.

A highlight of my year at Normal School was a trip to Victoria. Three other student teachers and I represented our school in a badminton tournament against the Victoria Normal School. We traveled on the old Princess steamboat, another first for me. We left at night and arrived in Victoria first thing in the morning. This is a bit different from a trip on a high-speed ferry which now travels from Vancouver to Victoria in less than 2 hours.

In early April, the flowers were all out in Beaconhill Park, about two weeks earlier than in Vancouver. We visited the legislature buildings, Helmcken House, and the museum. Royal Roads Cadets in red uniforms added excitement to the dance we attended. It was a glorious weekend. I do not remember if we won our games, but I resolved I would live in Victoria one day. This goal took many years to come true.

Practicum at Sexsmith Elementary School 1949

Graduation from Normal School was similar to that from high school, but on a more lavish scale. After the graduation ceremony, we had a banquet in the Georgia Hotel, which was very posh at that time. Of course, I had to have a new evening gown. It was mauve satin with a sweetheart neckline and a large bow on one hip. I only wore it once as it met a dreadful fate at the banquet.

Waiters, inexperienced I believe in retrospect, carried large silver trays with the entrees stacked upon them. Our meal consisted of roast beef with Yorkshire pudding and oven roasted potatoes, brown and delectable. As the waiter hovered with his tray just above me, a potato rolled off, bounced on my bosom, and cascaded down the front of my dress, leaving a trail of grease which never did come out. For the sake of politeness, I pretended I could not see any sign of damage to my dress, but it was painfully evident.

Our group of friends decided we would all go to Prince George District together the following year. I was offered a job teaching in a one-roomed school in the district, but at the last minute, I decided it was not the place for me to teach and I accepted a position in Langley. The other seven all went north together.

Graduation – 1949

68

Teaching in Langley
1949-1952

I accepted a position to teach in the Langley School District, in preference to other offers I had for Lillooet, Prince George, Abbotsford and Mission, mainly because Langley was one of the few districts, which paid women on the same salary scale as men. It was still common for men to be paid considerably more than women were, as men needed to support a family and women worked "just as a hobby". My starting pay was $1500 a year, paid in 10 instalments at the end of each month of school. From the end of June until the end of September, I received no cheque. A teacher was expected to manage his money carefully and save for the summer. My actual salary was thus $125 a month, less deductions, when calculated over 12 months.

Immediately after the war, Langley began to grow and there was no place to stay. Eventually I found an apartment above Ayres Second Hand Store. It was rented furnished, but I am sure the furniture was what they could not sell. There were four suites in the building with a shared bathroom at the end of the hall.

A few days after finding this treasure, I met another teacher,

Rachel Rosman, who was also looking for a place to stay and she moved in with me to share the rent.

Across the hall lived two waitresses who entertained visitors all hours of the day and night. Trucks would screech to a halt, and men's footsteps came up the outside stairs of the building. The men often mistakenly knocked, at our door which was the closest to the entrance. I was terrified, but Rachel was fearless.

"Irene?" they'd say, looking us up and down.

"No, look across the hall," Rachel would answer as I cowered behind her.

Langley from the air – 1951

After about 20 minutes, Rachel could not stand the suspense any longer.

"I think I should go next door and borrow some sugar," she would say.

With cup in hand she would knock on their door and make her request, quickly getting as good a look as she could at their activities.

We never became good friends with Irene and her roommate, but we grew to know a lot about her friends and her habits.

January 1950 was one of the coldest years on record. All the pipes and water connections at school burst and school was cancelled for the month of January. The School Board told teachers they were not allowed to leave Langley, as school might reopen any day. We were sure this was not going to happen.

Rachel and I were miserable in Ayre's Paradise, as we called our apartment. We had an oil range which stood near the kitchen window. Snow blew in from cracks around the window frame and remained in piles on the floor beside the stove, which did not give off enough heat to melt the snow.

Ayres' Paradise
X marks our apartment

In the next room, we had a double bed that we shared. Each day we dressed in our winter clothes, coats, gloves, scarves and hats and spent the day in bed trying to keep warm. Although the schools remained closed for the entire month, it was two weeks before the Board relented and we were able to leave Langley and return to our parent's homes to wait out the winter freeze-up.

In the spring, we found an apartment in a small triplex. We were its first tenants and it was clean, warm, nicely furnished and had its own bathroom, which we shared with another teacher in the adjoining apartment. Besides all these advantages, it was close to Langley Central School.

My first assignment was to teach Grade Four. Throughout the summer, I began to prepare lessons and get organized for my new class. However, on the first day of school I learned I was actually to teach Grade Five. As I was the "new kid on the block," I was given the lower division of students. An experienced teacher was assigned the top achieving Grade Five class. All the children with learning difficulties or behaviour problems were assigned to the beginning teacher. It would have been fairer to divide the classes randomly, but that was not the way it was done.

Arriving on the first day of school, I went into a classroom and was talking to another teacher I had known casually at Normal School.

The principal, Fred Cudlip, came into the room, looked at me and said, "Don't you think you should go out to play with the other children until the bell rings?"

"But, I'm Miss McDonald, the new teacher," I stammered.

Then it was his turn to be embarrassed.

School did not begin well. Because I was the youngest teacher on staff, I became the PE teacher for the senior girls. This was a challenge in a school without a gym. At Normal School, we were taught games to play in the classroom that were supposed to be fun and yet did not make sufficient noise to disturb the class next door. We played such games as relay races with chalk brushes and did callisthenics beside our desks. In fair weather, we went out onto the playground. During my first PE class, a girl tripped and fell on the field and broke her leg.

Later the same week, I heard a thud as a girl dropped from her desk onto the floor and began to thresh about and froth at her mouth. At Normal School, we had been taught what to do if a student had an epileptic seizure, but I hoped I would never have to deal with this problem. However, I did know what to do, and the student was not injured. There was no known treatment for epilepsy. Epileptics were looked upon with disdain, if not fear by many.

Each week I took my class roller-skating to a rink several blocks from the school. In my class was a boy, Eddie, who had a clubfoot. His parents would not permit him to have surgery to cure it, as they believed it was God's will for him to be born with this deformity. I wondered what to do with Eddie when the class went to the rink, but my worries were unfounded. Eddie clamped the skates on his running shoes and was soon speeding around the rink as fast as anyone else was.

Upon graduation from Normal School, I received a Temporary First Class Certificate. This permitted me to teach grades one to eight in any BC school. In order to have a Permanent First Class Certificate, a teacher was required to teach two years, have two satisfactory inspector's reports and successfully complete two years at Summer School.

A visit from the School Inspector was a frightening experience. Teachers told their students to be on their best behaviour when the Inspector arrived, as the students were encouraged to believe he was watching them. In truth, the Inspector was not only watching the teacher; but also evaluating and judging. He had the teacher's future in his hands.

First year teachers were the most vulnerable and the first on the Inspector's list to visit. After discussing every aspect of a teacher's lessons and the organization of her room and her unit plans, he would leave with a long list of everything she must do for improvement before he returned for a follow up visit. Later, a written report was sent to the teacher, the principal and to the Board. Copies were also filed with the Department of Education. My first report was sent to Abbotsford to my parent's address. When I visited them, Mother and Dad handed me an opened report. They said they could not wait for me to come home to see how I had managed as a first year teacher.

The report began, "Miss McDonald is doing well for a first year teacher." This last phrase tells it all. The first year is really in many ways a practice year. We all made many mistakes, but, hopefully, learned from them and carried on.

Following my first year as a teacher, I went to summer school in the old Victoria High School building. Mother and Dad were worried about where I would stay in Victoria so Dad arranged that I would board with a former girl friend of his, Kate. Her niece was also going to summer school so we arranged to meet and travel on the boat together. Lorraine had been in the army and was much older and worldlier than I was.

When we got to Aunt Kate's, there did not appear to be anyone at home.

"But she is expecting us," Lorraine said. "We'll just walk in as the door is not locked."

We wandered through the house and eventually found Aunt Kate asleep on a couch in the den. Lorraine leaned over, and touching her aunt on the shoulder, awakened her.

Kate shot up, "Who the hell are you?" she shouted, not knowing me and not recognizing Lorraine, at first.

At last, she got her bearings. "Well," she said, "We don't have any food in this house, but I'll buy you all a drink."

I certainly did not drink and I was getting quite hungry. Off we went to the kitchen and Aunt Kate opened the cupboards. There really was no food, but every shelf was filled with liquor. I spent the night there, but knew I had to find somewhere else to stay immediately.

After morning classes I stopped in a corner store near the entrance to the school and asked an elderly lady if she knew of any place in the area that might take a student. We talked for a few minutes. She said her daughter was a teacher, but not living at home at the time and I could have her daughter's room above the store for the summer. A great friendship developed between Mr. and Mrs. Andrews and me. I stayed with them for the two summers that I went to school in Victoria and we kept in contact for many years. They treated me like a granddaughter.

The second year I went to Summer School I decided to go by airplane. I did not know anyone (at the time) that had ever been in a plane except airmen during the war, and I thought it would be an exciting adventure. I flew from Vancouver airport, over the Fraser Delta, and on to Victoria. I remember, with amazement, the view, as I could recognize from the air, how soil was carried down the Fraser and deposited at its mouth to form islands.

At the end of teaching for two years and two years at summer school in Victoria, I was issued a Permanent First Class Certificate. Now I had, I believed, lifelong financial security, as the certificate could not be revoked.

Courtship and Marriage

After a month's closure in January, the schools eventually reopened. Rachel, my roommate, taught at Glenwood School, about five miles into the country. The school was sponsoring a whist drive to raise money for school activities and Rachel persuaded me to accompany her. We dressed up in our finest clothes with fancy open-toed sandals, and set out by taxi. About half a mile from the school, the taxi got stuck in the gravel road which was a quagmire following the spring break up.

"Well, girls," the taxi driver said as he opened the car door. "You'll have to walk the rest of the way."

As we stepped out, the cold mud covered our fancy shoes. We trudged through the dark, each step squishing, and splashing mud farther and farther up our legs. We had to press forward as there was nowhere to stop. We worried not only if we would ever reach the school, but also how we would ever get home. When we finally reached the school, we escaped to the washroom and tried to clean our legs with damp paper towels. We had minimal success. Luckily, once we got to a card table we could hide our legs under the tablecloth.

Ted and his parents had come to the school that evening to play cards. I did not even notice Ted. I was too self-absorbed by my muddy legs. He had seen us and after the party, he invited us to come to their farm to phone a taxi. I thought nothing more of the evening.

Once a week I played badminton in the community hall. The next time I went to the hall, Ted had also come to play. He reminded me that we had met at Glenwood School. From that time, we became good friends. We had many interests in common. Our first bond was our birthdays. Strangely, we shared the same birth date, May 8th, though Ted was born five years earlier than I, in 1925.

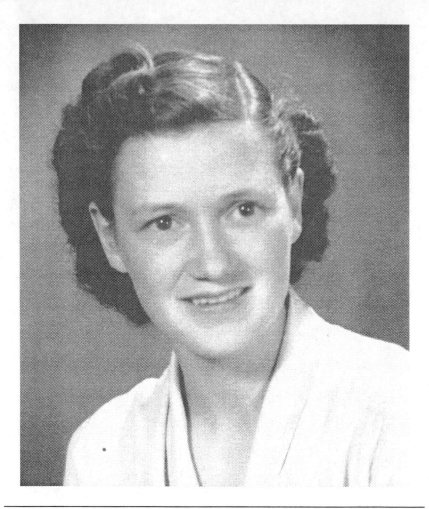

Joyce - 1951

Ted was great fun. He always treated me with kindness. He would open the car door, carry my parcels and was, in every way, a gentleman. At that time, he did not smoke or drink and he never used vulgar language. Once when a swear word slipped out, he apologized sincerely. Besides, I thought he was very handsome.

He liked to have the exact setting for important occasions. We drove to Birch Bay and parked at the edge of the ocean where he proposed to me. I did not hesitate to accept. Later on my 21st birthday, Ted's mother made us a beautiful cake baked in a special pan in the shape of two hearts joined together. A friend decorated it with both our names. That evening Ted gave me a

76

diamond engagement ring. We planned to marry as soon as Summer School was over and I had my Permanent Certificate.

While I was at Summer School, Ted wrote and suggested I should buy a wedding ring in Victoria, as there would not be time to have one sized after I returned to Abbotsford. It seemed like a sensible idea. I went to Birks Jewellers and asked to look at wedding rings. The clerk jumped to the conclusion that I must "have to get married", as the expression was at that time, for those who found themselves "in the family way". I could feel the contempt in her voice, as she looked me up and down and mentally tried to calculate how many months I was along. The thought had never crossed my mind that shopping for a ring could cause me so much embarrassment.

I chose a ring similar to my mother's ring, white and gold, with engraving. It cost $17, expensive for a ring without precious stones when most wedding rings were $5. I put the signature blue Birks box in my purse and slunk out of the store. I am not sure if Ted ever repaid me for that ring.

This is the account of our wedding, which appeared in the local paper, The Abbotsford News:

Residence in Langley Prairie Follows Wedding

The marriage of Mary Joyce McDonald to Ted Raymond Brown took place Wednesday, August 8, in the manse of the United Church here. Rev. Harold P. Marston officiated. The bride is the elder daughter of Mr. and Mrs. Harry A. McDonald, and the groom is the youngest son of Mr. and Mrs. Frederick (It should have said Fred) Brown, Langley Prairie.

The bride chose a white ballerina length gown of taffeta with Chantilly lace and matching bolero. She wore a chapel length veil of imported Swiss lace, which fell from a satin Juliet cap. Her bouquet was of pink roses and carnations.

Ruth McDonald was her sister's sole attendant. She chose a yellow nylon ballerina length gown with matching floral headband. Her bouquet was of colonial style made up of apricot carnations.

George Brown, Whalley, acted as his brother's best man. Only the immediate family attended the reception, held on the lawn of the bride's home.

Ted Raymond Brown -- 1950

A three-tier cake centred the lovely lace covered table, and pink and white stocks completed the appointments. Mrs. D.J. McDonald, grandmother of the bride, poured, and servitors were Mrs. J. McDonald, Penticton, Mrs. J. Webster, and Mrs. D. McDonald, all aunts of the bride. Jim Webster proposed the toast to the bride, answered by the groom.

Following the reception, the bride presented her bouquet to her grandmother. For traveling to Seattle, where the couple was going on their honeymoon, the bride wore a grey English suit with white accessories, and a corsage of pink carnations.

Mr. and Mrs. Brown will reside at Langley Prairie.

When it was time for us to go to the manse for the wedding, there was no groom. In fact, there were no Browns. After half an hour, my dad began to lose his composure.

He kept saying, "Are you sure he's coming?" as he had another drink. I was sure, but I was getting nervous.

Dad, Mother, Joyce, Ted
Rhoda & Fred Brown, Elsie & Duncan McDonald

Eventually George, Ted's brother, arrived with my grandparents. He had gotten lost in trying to find our house and had stopped to ask an elderly couple walking on the road for directions to our home. Grandma and Grandpa got in George's car and directed them. Later, the rest of the Browns arrived. Bill, Ted's other brother, had had car trouble and Ted and his dad had gone back to rescue him. As we finally got to the manse, the minister was just ready to leave as he thought we had decided not to get married.

Ted's mother had painful bunions and usually wore soft canvas shoes. She had a particularly comfortable pair that she wore to work in the garden. Imagine her horror when she looked down at her feet at the wedding and realized she had forgotten to put on her new shoes to match her wedding outfit.

George Brown, Best Man
Ruth McDonald, Maid of Honour

August 8, 1951

Who took the keys? -- Off to Seattle

My uncles thought it would be fun to phone the Canadian Customs Office at Sumas where they thought we would be crossing the border on our way to Seattle. They reported that an older man was smuggling a young girl across the border and requested we be stopped and I should be returned safely to my parents. We ruined their plans, as we did not go through Sumas Customs, but instead we went to the Vancouver Hotel, the most prestigious at that time, and had a special dinner in the dining room. The organist played many songs just for us, "Always" and "Because" and similar romantic ballads.

When we got to our hotel room, I was embarrassed to discover that my uncles had somehow been able to tamper my suitcases without my knowledge. They had gone into the garden and filled my cases with various vegetables, tomatoes, green beans, and cucumbers which they tied together to represent various phallic symbols. Fortunately, they had not removed my clothes!

The day before we married, the government slaughtered the poultry on the Brown's farm. The chickens had been identified with Newcastle disease, a respiratory infection. Ted had contacted this infection in his eyes, so we had to treat them with eye drops every couple of hours during our honeymoon.

While in Seattle, we saw many cars with advertisements on their bumpers announcing Billy Graham at the Forum. His name was not well known in 1951. We thought he was a dance band. For the first time we saw synchronized swimming at the Sea Festival. We also saw the musical Show Boat, which was a newly produced movie.

Life on the Farm
1951-1956

Ted's father, Fred Brown, had to retire early from his job as head boom-man in Ocean Falls because of failing health. He bought a marginal piece of land; five acres with a small house, about five miles south of Langley, on what was then called the Berry Road.

Ted was in his first year at the University of British Columbia when his dad retired. It was Ted's dream to become a doctor. Clearly, this was now impossible as his family could not help support him and there were no student loans in those days.

Ted and Fred decided to go into the broiler business. It was a new concept in farming, raising birds quickly and placing them on the market at a very lightweight, between 2 and 2/12 pounds.

A new type of facility was designed and built with three different sized rooms in which to move the chickens as they grew. Ted and his dad did some contract booming in Port Melon to raise money for these buildings.

First, the day old chicks were placed in the brooder room, which held two thousand day- old chicks. They were raised in wire mesh cages stacked in several tiers. Electric heat controlled the temperature and huge fans kept the air fresh. The brooder room was spotlessly clean. The walls were lined with gyproc and painted. Every effort was made to keep the room free of contamination. The men wore coveralls and made sure their shoes would not spread possible disease from the older birds to the chicks.

Power outages were common. A loss of heat or ventilation could soon result in the death of the birds, so Ted installed a backup power system. An enormous red fire alarm about 12 inches in diameter was mounted on a wall in the bedroom. The alarm sounded clearly in the poultry barns, quite some distance from the house. When the alarm went off, most often in the middle of the night, Ted would jump out of bed as if attacked, and hit the floor running to the barn. You can imagine how, in later years, our babies responded to that piercing sound.

Rhoda & Fred Brown, Tom & Diane
Christmas 1954

At two and a half weeks of age, the birds were mature enough to be moved out of the brooder room to the next larger room. The brooder room was then cleaned in preparation for the next batch of chicks. We had a huge steam cleaner for this purpose. The amount of space each chicken required to mature without overcrowding was carefully calculated. Overcrowding caused chickens to cannibalize each other, and this caused a loss of profit.

Later, the chickens were moved to the finishing room, which again, allowed the chickens more space as they continued to grow. In about eight weeks, the birds were ready to market. The men would get up at about four a.m. to catch the chickens before they (both the men and the chickens) were fully awake, put the birds in cages, and transport them to Vancouver to be sold.

The chickens were fed with an automatic watering system and the cages were emptied of manure with a conveyor belt. A screen was placed under the cages to catch the droppings. This screen was in turn covered with black building paper. A crank moved the belt along and the manure went directly into a wheelbarrow or container for the tractor to spread the manure on the fields. Manure did not have to be handled manually.

Both of these ideas were new at the time and invented by Ted and his dad. Researchers came from the U of BC and various research centres in United States to see how our farm operated. Several farm papers and "The Farm Broadcast" on CBC featured our farm.

In 1951, it was one of the largest broiler operations in Canada. 2000 day-old chicks were received every three weeks. Now farmers raise thousands of birds at a time in huge operations, where the birds are raised on the floor and not moved at various stages of their development.

The poultry business was devastated in 1951 by an outbreak of Newcastle disease, a respiratory disease for which there was no prevention or cure. On the day prior to our marriage, the government came to the farm and gassed all the chickens. The corpses were taken and sold for fat. There is not much fat on young birds One can imagine how much payment was received for them! There is not much fat on young birds. The farm was quarantined for several months while everything was steam cleaned and otherwise prepared for another batch of birds. In the next two years, we repeated this process twice more.

Eventually a vaccine was developed to prevent Newcastle disease. Each chicken was vaccinated when it was one day old, by placing a drop of vaccine into its eye. Ted and I got very efficient at this job. When the chickens were delivered, we would take them one at a time from the box in which they were packed. We held each chick securely, and using a syringe, carefully place one drop of vaccine into the corner of the chicken's eye, making sure that the chick did not move at exactly the wrong moment. Working together, Ted and I could vaccinate 1000 chicks every hour. This method of vaccination proved to be successful and we had no further incidents of this disease.

A year or two later, an improvement in the vaccine permitted the farmer to spray the vaccine into the brooder room instead of doing each bird manually. This was an example of another job specialty no longer in demand due to modern technology. Chicken vaccinators were highly paid.

Soon after we were married, I realized that I was pregnant. This created a financial problem, as I had to resign as soon as it became visually apparent that I was expecting a baby. Women used to wear their bulky winter coats when they went shopping, even in the summer, to cover evidence of their expanding waistlines. It was considered inappropriate for students to see a pregnant woman in the classroom. I continued to teach until the Easter break in April 1952.

Diane is very punctual now, but she delayed her arrival by two weeks, arriving finally on the 15th of August 1952. Each day after the due day, I defrosted the refrigerator and scrubbed the kitchen floor in anticipation of going to the hospital, but nothing happened. We did not have a car so Ted went to Abbotsford after supper on August 14th, to borrow Ian's car for the inevitable trip to the hospital.

As soon as Ted left, labour began. Shortly after, a friend of Ted's mother came to see me. I do not know why, as she was never pleasant to me, and I felt no friendship for her. She stayed for several hours and I never let on that I was in discomfort. When Ted got home, we left immediately for the hospital.

After many hours of labour, I was given ether, an anaesthetic, and remembered nothing of the birth until several hours after delivery. When the nurse brought Diane to me for the first time, I was shocked to see a long red mark from her temple, across her eye, and ending in a large burn on her cheek. The doctor had used forceps to help pull her into this world. He assured me the burn would heal in a few days, but it must have been deeper than he thought as Diane still has a scar.

Catherine Diane was a beautiful baby, all seven pounds nine ounces, with dark eyes and a dusting of dark hair. Great Grandma Pridmore made Diane and each of my following children white flannelette nighties from the same pattern that she had used for her own babies, and later for my siblings and me. Grandma hand stitched them with French seams and applied featherstitch embroidery around the necks. The nighties tied with two sets of ribbons at the back. I made each baby a knitted sweater, booties and a bonnet to come home from the hospital. Diane's outfit was white wool with a silver twisted thread.

The first night I was home with the baby I was afraid to go to sleep.

"What if I did not hear her cry in the night?" "What if she stopped breathing?" "What if..."

I had so many fears. Finally I thought to myself, "Other parents must sleep sometime." I turned over and fell asleep, exhausted. I was never so silly in this respect again.

The Brown family had many grandchildren, but Diane was the first for my parents and also the first great-grandchild for both of my sets of grandparents. On the night Diane was born, my dad and brothers were playing softball and the announcement came over the PA system that dad was a grandfather. The crowd cheered. There are not many men still competing on a ball team at age 45.

My parents often took Diane to stay with them before she went to school. Whenever they came to visit, Diane would get her little suitcase out and begin to pack it so that she could go home with them.

*4 Generations – Catherine Diane
Duncan McDonald, Joyce, Dad*

Diane was a very mature and responsible child. She liked to be a little mother to the children that followed her.

To supplement our income, especially when the farm was shut down because of Newcastle disease, Ted got a job as a salesman for a hatchery. Through this contact, we met Doug Gardiner and his family, whom Ted mentored into the chicken business. From this developed a life- long friendship. The Gardiners, who were recent immigrants from Scotland, belonged to a Scottish Country Dancing club. We used to go dancing frequently and soon could do "The Gay Gordons" and other traditional dances with abandon.

Thomas Frederic Brown arrived June 3rd 1954. I worried that I would not be able to look after two babies.

"How could I possibly look after a second child when one child took all of my time?" I wondered.

4 Generations – Diane- age 4 months
Mother, Joyce, Thomas Pridmore

This time, though, I witnessed my baby's birth and even more. Tom was a big baby, eight pounds six ounces, and was by far my most difficult delivery. It had become fashionable to have a natural childbirth. The use of ether was discouraged as recent research indicated its use might affect the baby, as well as the mother adversely. Queen Elizabeth had used a new product, Trilene, which the patient could control as required for pain. I was given an atomizer of this drug to hold and self-administer. At the foot of the bed was a large mirror where I could watch the delivery. I was fascinated. As soon as Tom was born, I sat up to get a better view of everything going on.

"Mrs. Brown," said the doctor. "Would you like to cut the cord?" This I did.

Later I was told to lie down to deliver the afterbirth. Then I sat up again and the doctor showed me the placenta, described all its parts and their functions, and explained how important it was

91

that all the parts be expelled. It was the most interesting biology lesson I have ever had.

Because of the pressure on Tom's head during delivery, it was severely misshapen. It came to not one point, but two humps like a camel's back. The doctor reassured me that his head would resume a normal shape within a week or two, but it took much longer than that.

Both the grandmothers were sick when they saw Tom, as they thought he must surely be mentally defective. For over six months, I kept a cap on his head to prevent people from staring. He had such a cute face, soft red hair, intelligent eyes and then far, above these eyes, the little pointy, head.

When Tom was a year old he became seriously ill. Doctors could not determine what the matter was, and we took him to the hospital for observation. After three days there, Tom passed a red currant stool. This is the sure sign of an intussuception. This condition occurs when a part of the large intestine, sensing a nodule of some sort on its surface, gradually draws part of the small intestine down into its self. Doctor Chapin Keyes told us that because the condition was not diagnosed for several days and because Tommy's body was so small, there was virtually no chance that he could survive surgery.

"If he does survive," the doctor cautioned, "the intestines will likely never function normally."

Ted pleaded with the doctor to at least try to save Tom's life and the surgery proceeded.

When we got home from the hospital after the surgery Ted knelt and said probably the most powerful prayer of his life for our baby. After rising from his knees, he had a strong feeling that everything would turn out all right and that Tommy would live. We felt assurance and comfort. It was fully a week later that the surgeon told us that Tom would survive and his body would function normally.

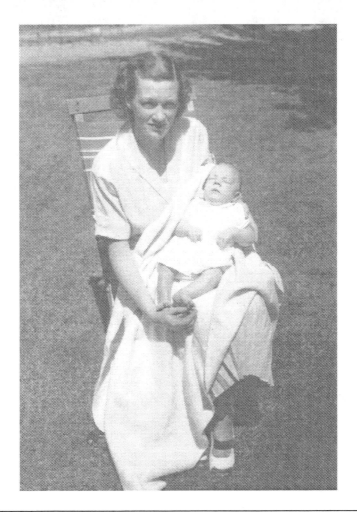

Joyce & Thomas Frederic – 6 weeks old

One of our neighbours was in the hospital at the same time as Tom. She was a young mother, dying of cancer. The nurses put Tom in bed with her each day and she held and comforted him as he gave her the comfort she missed from her small children. Although we visited Tommy each day, we could not stay with him. Hospital procedures, did not allow parents to stay with their children, except at specified visiting hours.

When Tommy came home, he clung to the yellow blanket he had in the hospital, which he named his Ki-Ki. It was never far from his hand. If I could snatch it away from Tom long enough to launder, he would stand under the clothesline, holding on to his blanket, and sucking his thumb.

Ted and I were concerned that Tom was too quiet and introverted when he was small. We did all we could to make him talk more, to be more outgoing. I think, in this respect, we succeeded. I do not think many people would now suggest that Tom needs to talk more. It is one of his gifts, to be able to express himself clearly and in an interesting manner.

During the time we farmed, we bought the five acres next to the farmhouse, which contained the little house we first rented. Ted's sister, Grace, lived there after we moved from it. Later, Ted and his dad bought the wooded five acres backing the farm, increasing its area to 15 acres. Much of the land was poor, quite gravelly and thin, but Ted added manure each year to the depth of several feet in some parts. By the time we left the farm, it had rich, heavy loam.

One year, after this land was cleared and built up, we decided to plant about two acres in strawberries. Ted worked very hard and planted them in the fall ready for the next spring's crop. That year, 1955, we had an early frost and then snow the first week of November. Five plants survived. We did not try strawberries again.

During the five years we farmed, circumstances forced us to move to several different houses up and down the Berry Road. When Diane was a baby, the hired hand's house on the Rees farm became available. It was a small, two-bedroom cottage, but it had indoor plumbing. What a luxury! We lived there about a year until the Rees' needed the house once more for their employee.

We then moved across the road from the farm to a two-storied house belonging to the Malik family. The house had running water and a path to the outhouse. This path flooded when it rained so we had to walk on wooden planks in our gumboots across the yard to the toilet for much of the year.

The house had a sawdust burner for heat and cooking. This was a great convenience compared to a wood range, as the burner gave steady heat. A regular wood stove was modified by having a large metal hopper welded to the side of the stove.

Trucks delivered loads of waste sawdust from the sawmill and dumped it into a shed near the house. Then we would carry the sawdust into the kitchen in large pails and dump it into the hopper. A lid on the hopper prevented dust from escaping into the kitchen as the fuel burned, but certainly not as it was being dumped. A damper controlled the speed at which the sawdust entered the stove to be burned. I would open this damper wider to increase the burning rate and thus control not only the temperature of the oven, but also of the entire house. There was a metal grill in the ceiling above the range to allow warm air to escape and warm the upstairs bedrooms.

A disadvantage was that the hopper was very hot near its base. Diane has a scar on the back of her hand where she touched the hopper. Another disadvantage was that often the sawdust would "hang up" in the hopper. When you thought the fire should be burning well, it was actually going out. From time to time, I would have to lift up the hopper lid and, with a tool specially designed for the purpose; poke at the sawdust to make sure it was dropping down where it could burn properly.

At this house, we had a wonderful garden. It had deep, dark soil, like bottomland. It was strange that across the road, our land was originally very poor and rocky. In the spring as I was preparing the garden for planting, I decided to light a little fire to burn off the browned grass. I thought it would be well controlled as the land was still quite wet. Before I knew it, the fire had spread over our whole yard and threatened to speed out of control down the road. Luckily the wind, which somehow picked up just as I got my fire going well, moved in the direction away from the house and no real damage was done.

Farmhouse on Berry Road

After about two years, we had to leave that rented house also. We then moved to the only house available, a house belonging to the Jones' family. It was the least attractive and most inconvenient house we ever lived in. The outside was unpainted and the inside had never been finished. There were bare wooden floors without linoleum. There was a well outside with a pump to get our water and, of course, no plumbing. We did buy an electric stove which Ted learned to wire in. This was the beginning of his electrical training.

After about a year in that house Ted's parents rented a house, a few blocks away and we moved into the farm house. It had a bathroom, hot and cold running water, and our electric stove. Although it was small, we had two bedrooms, a living room and a kitchen with an eating nook.

David Allen Brown was born November 29th, 1955. Like Tom, the previous year, David arrived just one day before his due date. I no longer worried about trivialities like having the refrigerator defrosted before going to the hospital, but rather concentrated on the mountains of laundry. It had rained almost steadily throughout November and my daily routine was concentrated on getting clothes dry. Before going to bed the night before David was born, I draped clothes on the backs of every chair, hoping they might be dry by morning. They were dry by the time I returned home a week later.

By poor management, the 29th of November was the day we shipped chickens to Vancouver. Ted got up about 4 a.m. to begin to catch the chickens and load them in the truck. He tried to catch them in the early morning while they still roosted. It really made things inconvenient when I reported I had to go to the hospital at about 6 a.m.

"I'll just drop you off and come right home," said Ted.

Fathers were not allowed to be with their wives in the delivery room, but they could remain in a special waiting area. There was nothing Ted could do in the hospital, so I agreed that he should go directly home, complete the chicken catching and return later. David arrived very quickly.

Following his delivery, the nurse said I could phone home and report on the baby's safe arrival. Direct phone dialling was not yet available. When I wanted to phone, I turned a crank at the side of the phone box. This alerted the telephone operator, who asked what phone number I wanted. She then manually connected the phone lines together. Each phone line had several customers, each identified by a specific ring. Our line had six other houses. Our ring was two longs and a short ring. Although I could hear everyone's phone ring, it was discourteous to pick up the phone when the ring identified the call was for another family, though many people did listen in to other's calls.

I lifted the telephone receiver and asked the operator for our phone number. Getting Ted on the phone, I said, without identifying myself,

"It's another boy."

"Who is this calling?" Ted asked.

He could not believe the baby had been born in the length of time it took him to drive back to the farm.

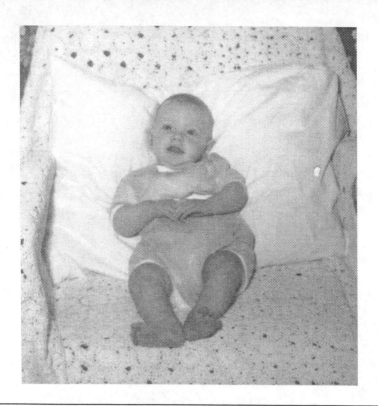

David Allen - 3 months old

A few days after we came home from the hospital, I noticed that David had ugly sores around his unhealed navel. The doctor told me that it was staph infection and he had likely contacted it in the hospital. I removed all his clothes each time I changed him and with his receiving blanket, put everything on the stove in a large preserving pot filled with water, soap and bleach. I boiled every item for 20 minutes or longer. I carried the procedure to ridiculous extremes, continuing the routine for several weeks, but the infection did not spread. Some babies whose mothers were not careful had most of their babies' bodies covered with boil-like infections, and some babies died.

The farm was not able to support two families so in 1956, Ted and I, with our three small children, left the farm to his parents and set off on our own. Ted's parents moved back to the Berry Road and continued to farm for a few years, eventually selling the farm and retiring to Newton, Surrey.

Tom, Joyce & David, Diane -- 1956

Tom, Ruth McDonald, Diane

Penticton
1956-1957

Ted got a job with Mutual of Omaha selling health and accident and life insurance. His territory was to be the interior and northern areas of BC, with his base in Penticton.

In Omaha, where Ted went for training, he saw the original computer used by the company to keep their records. It was several stories high and probably had less capability than a modern laptop. Ted could immediately see the potential of this technology.

We spent about six months in Vancouver, as Ted completed extensive training with an experienced agent. We left in the spring for Ted's new career.

We packed all our possessions in the back of the farm pick-up and moved with our three children, to the Okanagan. Ted bought a new station wagon, the first vehicle we owned. There were no vacant houses in Penticton in the tourist season, so we rented a summer cottage at Kaleden, on Okanagan Lake.

It was late to plant when we arrived, but we decided to put in a garden anyway. We had never seen crops grow so fast. Between our house and the next door neighbour's was a cement retaining wall which held the day's heat and released it during the night. We planted corn close to the wall. Every morning when we looked at the corn, we could see how many inches it had grown overnight.

There were five peach trees in the garden and we feasted on the fruit. Just one bite of the peach, the juice poured out and I had to wash my arms. There was so much fruit, but we could not even give it away. We also feasted on asparagus. In earlier years, asparagus was planted in the orchards as a cover crop, and later it spread along the roadsides and the railway tracks. We would go out and pick it by the pailsful.

Ted
Mutual of Omaha staff photo

One day shortly after we arrived, I hung my washing out on the clothesline. A squall came up and I rushed out to grab my laundry as fast as possible. My neighbour told me later that it was the funniest thing she had ever seen. I did not know that it would rain for only a short time and then the clothes would dry in only a few minutes in the intense Okanagan sunshine.

In early fall Uncle Joe, who lived in Penticton, found us a rental house on Tennis Street, right downtown. This was very convenient as Ted was away much of the time and I had no vehicle.

Shortly after we moved to Penticton, Tom disappeared. We searched everywhere. Our neighbours joined in the search and Ted took our car around the nearby streets searching for him, but all in vain. Eventually we heard an announcement on the radio about a small boy matching Tommy's description found in a downtown store. He had been exploring on his tricycle, eventually arriving at a florist shop where the staff realized a three year old should not be out alone. They took him into their premises.

When asked his name he said, "I'm Tom, Tom, the piper's son."

The staff was trying to find Petersons in the phone book before Ted finally rescued him.

Ted did very well as an insurance salesman. For several months, he was the top salesman in Canada, but other months he did less well. We never knew how much money we would have and Ted had the expenses of travelling, hotels and meals on the road.

On one occasion, Ted had been away for several weeks and I had not had any money. We had almost nothing in the house to eat. For lunch, I had made biscuits with jam. I was not sure what tomorrow would bring unless I soon received money in the mail. Uncle Joe came to tell me my mother and dad were coming to visit the next day. (We had no telephone.) I did not know what to do. I would never tell them we were having financial trouble. That would be disloyal to Ted. I knew they would have gone out and bought me groceries if they had known our situation, but I was too proud to tell them.

Fortunately, the next day Uncle Joe said my parents had phoned him and cancelled their planned trip. I was so relieved. That day, also, I received a cheque from Ted and life returned to normal.

The house in Penticton was comfortable and convenient. There was a gas water heater, which needed to be lit with a match when hot water was required. Burning of gas, however, created quite a bit of humidity in the air. There was an enclosed porch off the kitchen. When it was cold in the winter, this condensation from the propane would freeze on the back door so there was a block of ice several inches thick on the bottom 10 or 12 inches of the door, effectively freezing us into the house. After the first day, I learned to have an axe handy and each morning I chopped us out of the house. Luckily, the front door did not freeze closed so we could always have escaped in case of fire.

We did not plan to have any more children after David was born. We believed we could not afford more than three children. Foolishly, I   gave away my maternity clothes and baby equipment.

"Auntie" Jane Smith
80th Birthday

Karen Rose came along on April 7, 1957. I awoke early in labour that day and we raced off to the hospital. Despite the pleas of the nurse, Karen would not wait and she was delivered before the doctor arrived. Karen was a beautiful baby with blue eyes and very blonde hair, what little there was of it. We now had a perfect family: two boys and two girls.

On our way home from the hospital we stopped at Aunt Joyce's house to show off our new baby to her great-great aunt, Jane Smith. Auntie put a silver dollar in Karen's hand.

"It is the custom in England to cross a baby's hand with silver so she will never lack for anything in her life." One hopes this wish to be true in Karen's life.

Karen weighed seven pounds, two ounces at birth, but did not grow very quickly. At one year of age, she weighed only 19 pounds. Karen was, however, strong and active. She walked at about 10 months of age and could stand upright as she walked under the table.

Karen Rose – age 4 months, Diane

Before Karen was born, I read a book called "Karen", which was about a child who was born with cerebral palsy. Though doctors told her parents Karen would never reach adulthood, the family pulled her through many near-death experiences.

Because I was so impressed by Karen's fight for a normal life and by the support of her family, we decided to name our daughter in honour of this child and her courageous family. Our Karen has shown many of the desirable characteristics of this family.

Karen was always a gentle child. She would go to any lengths to have peace and harmony about her. Her brothers and sisters responded to her caring and loving manner, and each considered her a best friend. Although quiet and unassuming, Karen was competent in everything she tried to do.

Before the Christmas of 1957, Ted was working in the Quesnel area. He arrived home Christmas Eve with a generous Christmas bonus from his employer, which meant we had a more prosperous Christmas than we expected. Friends in Quesnel also gave him a hindquarter of moose. It was not cold enough to keep the moose frozen, so Christmas Eve found us cutting and canning this moose meat. We had only our kitchen knives and a cookbook showing the cuts of meat. It took us almost all night to wash jars, prepare the meat and process it, but meat was too valuable to waste and we were grateful for it.

It was during the time we lived in Penticton that we first met missionaries from The Church of Jesus Christ of Latter-day Saints. New missionaries had come to Penticton to open the area. They visited us several times and we were very interested in the message they brought. When they asked us to join the church, we said we had not made up our minds. They told us that they were only allowed to visit three times unless we made a commitment. When we did not make a commitment at that time, we did not see them again. This brief encounter was to have far-reaching implications 20 years later. I have often wondered how different our lives would have been if we had joined the church at that time.

Grandma & Grandpa McDonald
50th Wedding Anniversary
September 3, 1956

107

Mt. Lehman
1957-1959

In 1957 Ted's brother, Bill, established a logging business operating on the Fraser River at Mt. Lehman, not far from Abbotsford. During the year, logs were cut in the interior of B.C. and strapped into bundles. During the spring freshet, the bundles were dumped into the river and the power of the current transported them through the Fraser Canyon and into the calmer water close to the mouth of the river. A tug would put a grapple line on the bundle and tow it to shore. Here the heavy wires holding the bundles together were cut off and the logs were made into flat booms and towed to the mills. Bill's business was to catch these bundles and make them into booms.

Bill proposed that Ted be hired to run the tug for the company. The pay was $400 a month, a large sum at that time and about equal to what Ted earned as a salesman. He could be home all the time and would not have travel expenses. We decided to return to the coast. Ted was happy working on the river and we began to get ahead.

We rented a house on 10 acres of land in Mount Lehman, close to the river. We soon discovered it was also close to the mosquitoes. When the bundles were opened, black clouds of mosquitoes, breeding in the pockets of water held by the bundles, escaped in the thousands. The men could not see each other, even standing close together. Ted would dive into the river, not only to cool off in the summer, but also to get rid of the mosquitoes.

As our house was only half a mile away, we also were beleaguered with the insects. When I hung out the clothes, I wore gloves to try to keep them off my hands. Even then, I was in a black cloud. Fortunately, we had a full basement in the house so the children could play indoors in the summer months while the bugs were so bad. Insect repellent had not yet come onto the market.

Mrs. Roskewich's house, which we rented for $110 a month, was very attractive and modern. It had two bedrooms, a huge living room, a kitchen and bathroom. The floors were all hardwood and easy to keep clean. I would first apply a generous layer of Johnson's paste wax with a rag. Then I would give each of the children an old pair of Ted's wool socks; they would run and slide on the floors until they shone perfectly. It was great fun and a wonderful way to fill a summer day when they could not go out into mosquito territory.

Randy Pokeda, Karen, Diane David, Heather Brown, Tom
August 1957

Just beyond the back steps was a huge orchard with massive cherry, apple and pear trees. They were particularly good varieties and bore heavily. Along two fences were many plum trees. They had a kind of disease in the wood, called plum knot, that made the trees knarled, but the prune plums were prolific. I soon had all my jars full of fruit. The soil was excellent and we had a very good garden.

Karen loved all fruit, especially cherries. Many cherries fell to the ground, but they never stayed there. She kept the area completely clean of fallen fruit; not even a pit remained as she ate them,

110

stones and all. I hoped none of the fruit was rotten - Karen did not discriminate. Every cherry disappeared before anyone could check them out.

Wild blackberries grew prolifically along all the roads. One day Tommy and Diane were playing on a milk stand across the road from our house. I heard a blood-curdling scream. Tom, wearing the usual short pants, was on the ground beside the stand completely surrounded by blackberry vines. Each time he moved, he got more stabs from the sharp hooks. I ran and pulled him out, each of us attacked even more by the thorns. Tommy claimed Diane pushed him, but that was never clearly established.

When the first logging season ended in November, we received devastating news. Ted had been told that there was no need to pay into Unemployment Insurance. He was considered a manager; his salary would continue through the winter even if, or when, the operation closed. One day, without warning, we discovered that there was no work. Worst of all, there would be no income.

Mrs. Roskewich said we could pay our rent in the spring when logging started again. For the first and only time in our lives, we charged our groceries for the four months Ted was off work. Luckily I had done a lot of canning and we were very careful not to buy anything except the most basic and inexpensive foods from the store. It took us several months to repay these debts.

During this lay-off, Ted made us a bedroom suite, consisting of a bed and two dressers. Ted also made a set of bookcases that we used as a divider, making a bedroom from one end of the living room. Ted also made three little wooden wheelbarrows, painted red, so our three oldest children could help in the garden.

For Christmas Tommy had received a wooden model of a double-decker bus. Later we heard him call out as he looked out the window, "Mom, Dad, come right now, there is a double-decker rabbit outside." This was Tom's first lesson about the facts of life.

We lived close to nature in Mt. Lehman. One summer day we had all gone outside for a few minutes, leaving the kitchen door open.

When we came back in, a small bird was sitting on the table eating lettuce from a salad bowl, that that was left out.

David, Tom, Diane
Hallowe'en 1957

One day when David went out to play, he told me he was going hunting for an elephant and would bring it home.

"That's nice," I said encouragingly and thought no more of it.

In about an hour, he came back into the house carrying the remains of a toy elephant that some other child must have buried in the ground.

"I knew there was an elephant in our yard," he said. Never doubt the faith of a child.

The children liked to look in Ted's lunch tin when he came home from work, to see if there were any leftovers that they could eat before suppertime. Imagine their surprise one day when they opened the tin and inside were three baby ducks. They had been

112

abandoned on the river; perhaps their mother was killed. We cared for them for many days, but eventually Ted returned them to the river.

One day Ted came home and announced that the river was low and many islands were showing up in the river. We would take the tugboat and our picnic supper and explore one of these sand bars. Off we went.

With the exception of Ted, none of us had ever been on a boat. My legs were quivering as I carried Karen and walked along a plank to get into the boat. I would rather have stayed on the boat with the baby than to try to get onto the island, but Ted insisted that I get off the boat and join the rest of the family. Eventually I did.

David – age 2 years

Diane, Tommy and David were fearless. They had a wonderful time steering the tugboat, peering at the wake and scampering over the sand dunes. I envisioned them swept out to sea, but they were perfectly safe. I hoped I would never have to go on a boat again. Little did I know what was to come later.

About once a month, I would take the children on the bus to Abbotsford. "One single fare to Abbotsford," I would say as the five of us went to spend the afternoon at Mother's. Preschool children did not pay.

People would say to me, "But they're not all yours, are they?" when they saw how close in age the children were.

Baptism day for Karen & David -- Ted & Karen, Joyce & David
Tom, Diane -- 1957

"Are you a Catholic?" "That's disgusting to have so many children.", or even worse comments not fit for a family book. I did not share their view.

We attended the little pioneer United Church in Mt. Lehman where David and Karen were baptized. The Christmas concert at the church was a major community event. When Tom was three, he recited the poem "What Can I Give Him" (Poor as I Am). I did not think it unusual for a child that age to be able to recite in front of an audience, but the people there were very impressed by Tom's poise and maturity.

Diane began school in Mt. Lehman walking the half mile back and forth each day. Diane loved every day at school and talked constantly about all the exciting experiences she had. A new authority, who knew absolutely everything, her teacher, dominated Diane's conversation.

Arlene Ruth – age 15 months
Grandma Brown

One day Ted, opening a jar of beets using a knife, received a deep cut to his hand. He had some stitches and an anti-tetanus shot and we thought little more of it. A few days later, he collapsed with an allergic reaction to the vaccine.

I ran about a quarter of a mile in the middle of the night to phone for a doctor. It is not easy to run when almost nine months pregnant. Our neighbour drove Ted to the hospital in Abbotsford. Throughout the night the nurses gave him alternate shots of adrenaline and cortisone every 20 minutes to try to bring him safely through this crisis.

When I talked to Dr. Cannon the next day, he told me that Ted would live, but for most of the night, they had almost given up hope for his survival.

Arlene Ruth was due to arrive March 10, 1958 but stubbornly waited until exactly a month later, to the day. The doctor told me I was expecting twins. There were no ultra-sound or other testing techniques; I accepted the word of the doctor. I grew enormously large, weighing 150 pounds. I could not even do up the buttons on my maternity clothes after gaining 40 pounds.

Arlene was my easiest delivery despite the fact she was the largest, weighing eight pounds, 14 ounces. What a relief to discover there were no twins, just one large and very active child.

When I told my mother that I had virtually no pain with Arlene's delivery, she said, "Don't be silly. Everyone suffers."

Arlene never seemed like a newborn baby, but like a month-old child. She was strong, alert and grew very quickly. At four months of age, she was the same weight as Karen and, at a year, weighed over 30 pounds. It seemed as if she and Karen were actually twins, though Arlene was the bigger one.

Feeling our future was secure and Ted was earning a good income, we decided to build a house in Aldergrove. It was still close to Ted's work in Mt. Lehman, but away from the mosquitoes that kept the children indoors for two months of the year.

We bought a property in downtown Aldergrove and Ted began construction. The house had three bedrooms, a kitchen and large

116

living room. The most attractive feature was a floor-to-ceiling red brick chimney, with a raised slate hearth. When the house was liveable, we moved in, deciding to finish it as we could afford to.

Grandpa & Grandma Pridmore
Arcola, 1957

Aldergrove
1959-1961

While we lived in Mt. Lehman Ted had gone to night school and got his electrician's license. This allowed him to legally wire our house. Later, he took further courses and upgraded his certification so he could do electrical contracting. All was going well.

This was not to last. Bill's business, which we felt was secure, failed and he declared bankruptcy. Again, Ted was out of work. The general economy was depressed and Ted could not find a steady job. He did get some electrical contracting work, but it was erratic and people were slow to pay their bills.

Some people wanted to pay in creative ways. A customer contacted Ted. Bill Snow (I will never forget his name) knew he was going to die soon and wanted to leave his wife as well cared for as possible. He needed some wiring to upgrade his house and make it more comfortable for her. Ted worked about three days on the contract and it finally came time to settle his account. We needed groceries desperately and I was eager for Ted to come home with his pay.

When Ted came home at suppertime, he was carrying two bird cages. "Now, just let me explain," Ted said.

When the work was done, the customer said, "Let me show you my birds."

He took Ted downstairs where he had two Hartz Mountain canaries. These were the last two of his show birds and they were not only well loved, but also very valuable: they were the best of his breeding stock.

"Won't you take my birds in exchange for your electrical work?" Bill had said.

"What could I do?" Ted said to me. "The man is dying."

"I'd rather have money," I said coldly, thinking of my bare cupboards.

Of course, Ted was right. The man was dying; we still had other opportunities to prosper.

The birds were beautiful. The male was a deep orange colour, the female yellow. They would sing for long periods with the most beguiling warbles and triple trills one could imagine. They brought us much pleasure.

Shortly after we acquired the birds, Grandpa and Grandma Pridmore came to visit for a few days. Grandpa was a bird fancier and had raised birds in England. He knew what to do. He would teach us how to breed the birds.

Grandpa made all the necessary preparations. A little nest was constructed from cotton batting, egg yolk was mashed and put in the cage, and special feed was added to the cage for the female. All was ready.

That night, before we went to bed, we put the male in to keep her company and do what he surely knew how to do.

When we got up, we could not hear any singing. There was no sound from the cage. There, lying on the floor of her cage was the new husband, stone cold and stiff, his little legs pointing upwards.

On another occasion, Ted had done some wiring in a dairy barn. A few days later, we got an irate phone call from the farmer. His cow had died and he was going to sue Ted for its loss. X-rays showed the cow had eaten pieces of wire, which punctured its stomach, causing death. The farmer accused Ted of not cleaning up bits of wire as he worked. We were sick with worry.

We could hardly go from day to day. A lawsuit would have been devastating. We contacted a veterinarian friend, Trevor Clarkson, who said cows were always finding pieces of nails and other

120

metal objects. He added that the farmer was just looking for an easy target to reclaim the expenses of his loss. We never heard from the farmer again, but he did cause us a great loss of sleep.

There was little fighting in our home. Our children were taught to settle any disagreements in a peaceful way. As we did not live near other children in Mt. Lehman, this rule was easy to enforce. The children entered a new world when we moved to Aldergrove.

On the first day, the boys went outside to play. Before they even got off the porch, four boys from next door, armed with sticks embedded with nails, ran over to proclaim their territory - all of the free land between our two houses. Tom and David were terrified. They stood, quivering on the steps, too frightened to move. It took days before they felt free to move off the steps. Eventually, they became braver and even played with our neighbours, but there was never a great friendship.

Even at a very young age, Diane liked to cook. Once, when she was only about eight years old, she came home from school early, before I returned from the store, and decided she would bake an angel food cake. She went across the road to a farm where we bought fresh eggs and charged a dozen. Diane stirred them together with the other ingredients to make the cake. She did not have the technique down pat so we ate something like a baked angel omelette.

When David was about three years old, he went into the crawl space, where it was cool and dark, and fell asleep. We searched for him for hours before he woke up and came out completely unconcerned about our worries. He held in his hand a five dollar bill which someone must have lost under the house. He should have paid someone for the time and effort spent searching for him.

Behind our house was a vacant lot which was being levelled for a new subdivision. David not yet four years old, climbed on the bulldozer and managed to get it moving. He also got the bucket to raise and lower. I was horrified to look out the window and see David operating the equipment while all the neighbourhood children ran around the machine. I did not know what to do to stop the dozer, but managed to get a neighbour to come and put

121

an end to David's career as a heavy-duty equipment operator, at least for a few years.

After Arlene's birth, we knew we would not have any more children. For the second time, we gave away all of our baby equipment and clothes. At the beginning of 1960, the children began to nag us to have another sister as a Christmas present for the following year. Even the boys wanted a sister.

"We won't ask for anything else," they promise. "We just want a baby sister."

Ted and I kept telling them no, but they never let up their persistent pleas.

I should not have been surprised to discover that another baby was on her way (due date January 1, 1961). I would not go so far as to say she was planned, except by her brothers and sisters.

Like all the other girls, Susan Marie did not arrive on time. Finally, on Friday the 13th, I went to the hospital to be induced. Medication was put in a solution, which dripped into my arm intravenously. This brought about contractions and a quick birth.

When Susan was born, the umbilical cord was wrapped three times around her neck. It did not take the doctor long to grab her and unwrap the cord. There could have been serious damage to her brain if the oxygen supply had been cut off during delivery. Susan, weighing just over seven pounds, was a beautiful baby with brown eyes and quite a bit of thick, dark hair.

All the children fought to hold her or, as they said, "It's my turn to try out the baby."

Susan's feet never touched the ground. There was always someone to carry her. Susan did not like to cuddle, but would sit bolt upright on my knee. Perhaps she just got too much handling and cuddling.

Once when Aunt Joyce was visiting, Arlene asked her to play rummy. Aunt Joyce was just haphazardly passing Arlene cards as we talked together.

"No," said Arlene, "that is not how you play." She proceeded to show Joyce how to arrange the cards in suits, in threes and in runs.

Joyce had taught kindergarten for 40 years and could not believe a three year old was able to play a complicated mathematical game. We played cards with all our children. We were not surprised that even the younger ones could follow the rules.

We continued to struggle to make ends meet. Electrical jobs were scarce. The economy was depressed and so were we. Finally, we decided that I would have to return to work. I tried to get a position in Langley District, but there were no teaching jobs available in the Fraser Valley.

I accepted a position in Shearwater on the northern B.C. coast. Andy Widsten, whom Ted had worked for when he was a student in Ocean Falls, owned a marine business there. I did not want to return to teaching. I did not know how I could possibly work full-time with six small children. I was not thrilled with living so far north, but knew we could not survive any longer living as we were in the Fraser Valley. Naively, I thought if I taught for two years, I would be able to return to being a stay-at-home mom. It never happened.

We had no medical or dental insurance. The prenatal care and delivery of a baby cost $100.

For many years, we paid $10 a month to the doctor and another $10 to the dentist. By the time one pregnancy was paid for, it was time to start payments on the next. We were never able to catch up on these expenses.

Prior to going north, we all had the necessary dental work done. As David was to begin Grade One, I took him to the doctor for the required medical examination, including an eye exam.

The doctor said, after examining David, "Do you realize this child is almost blind?"

As a teacher, I had been taught to observe children carefully for evidence of various physical handicaps, but had not noticed anything different about David. I knew he could not do some of

123

the things Diane and Tommy had done at his age, but did not attribute that to his vision. I thought he was not developing as quickly as they had.

The first time he put on the thick glasses the doctor prescribed, he looked up at me and said, "Mommy, is that what you look like?"

Tears came to my eyes. Immediately, he could tie his shoes and do other tasks that required hand-eye coordination. The doctor told me David would likely be blind before he was an adult but, fortunately, this did not prove to be true.

David always had two, sometimes three, pairs of glasses en route back and forth to Vancouver for repair. Glasses were not meant for an active boy like him. His glasses were always held together with wire, toothpicks or tape. One pair was on its way to Vancouver, another was on its way back, and the third pair was held together waiting for its replacement to arrive.

Joyce & Arlene
David, Diane, Karen, Tom
1959

Shearwater
1961-1963

We left for Shearwater the day after Diane's birthday, August 16, 1961. With the exception of Ted, none of us had ever been on a large boat. It was exciting to climb into our berths in the stateroom and try to go to sleep. From the portholes, we watched the lights of Vancouver disappear as we sailed under Lion's Gate Bridge and into Burrard Inlet.

The next morning we went to the dining room for breakfast: another first for our children.

"And how many to sit at your table?" the steward asked Ted

"Nine," he replied as we had not only our six children, but also an older man, Richard, whom Ted had befriended and who was accompanying us north.

"But that is impossible," the steward said ungraciously.

However, he did sit six at one table with Susan in a high chair beside us. Richard and Tommy sat at a different table far from our view. Tom felt quite grown up and important.

As we traveled north, passengers kept saying, "Wait until you get to the Sound. Then you will be sick."

The children kept saying, "Are we there yet?"

Eventually we did get to Queen Charlotte Sound, an open area north of Vancouver Island, out of the protection afforded by the Inside Passage. Often the seas are rough and there can be a heavy swell, but on this day, there was not even the hint of a ripple on the water.

At last, the passengers could reply, "Yes, you're on the Sound now."

Immediately first one and then the next child became sea sick until five children were lying on their bunks, retching and crying. Susan, being only seven months old, did not understand she was supposed to be sick and continued to walk about the deck holding on to furniture and entertaining the other passengers. After some time in the crowded cabin, caring for the children, I could not do anything but join them in the misery of seasickness.

Susan Marie – age 1 year

There was no entertainment as you would expect on a cruise ship. This was a freight boat that carried some passengers. An elderly man did ask Ted to have a game of checkers with him in the evening. After about five moves, the game was over. It turned out the man was the Canadian Checkers champion. He did not ask Ted to play again.

When we woke up the next day and looked out the porthole there was absolutely nothing to see. We were travelling in heavy fog. It was too foggy to dock in Bella Bella so a fish boat came out to Llama Pass to pick up a newly graduated nurse who was coming to work at the United Church Mission Hospital. We all went through the galley (kitchen to the landlubbers) to watch her disembark. Heavy cargo doors were opened and we saw a little gill-netter bouncing up and down in the water. The nurse was expected to watch the boat's action and jump onto the rolling boat when it was conveniently even with the passenger ship.

"I can't do it," she declared. "I'm not going to Bella Bella. I'm going back home to Ontario."

Eventually, the fisherman carried her off the freighter and put her into his boat. Shortly they disappeared into the fog.

Later, Andy Widsten, the owner of the Shearwater Marina, came out in the Lady Marjory. We had to repeat the same routine as had the nurse, but no one carried me aboard. We struggled out of the galley with all our baggage and headed to BC Packers, Bella Bella.

The children were amazed to see a cow, destined for an isolated location, watching us with baleful eyes as we passed her en-route to the galley. I wondered how her owners would get her off into a fishing boat.

The tide was out when we arrived so we had to scale a ladder attached to the dock. It seemed to be about one hundred feet high and straight up. I suggested I would stay on board with the baby, but Ted insisted I go up the ladder first and he would catch me if I fell. I was so self- absorbed in my fright, I have no idea how we got all the children up on the dock.

Some bad news awaited us there. We had packed a trunk with the most essential items, bedding and dishes to do us until our belongings arrived by barge in a week or two. Somehow, it was not at Bella Bella when the freight was unloaded there. Luckily, Auntie Jean, as the whole camp called Andy's wife, supplied us with these items until our trunk was located. It had gone to Bella Bella Village and was soon delivered to us. Although both towns have the same name, they are on separate islands within sight on a clear day.

When we were ready to leave Bella Bella, we could not find Richard. He disappeared without a trace. Eventually we heard he had had a heart attack, had gone to the hospital, and then returned to Aldergrove on the next week's boat. We never heard of him again.

As we finally arrived at Shearwater, the fog began to lift and we saw what was to be our home for the next two years. We could see the sawmill to our right, as we approached the dock. Surrounding the mill and dropping into the ocean nearby, were piles of sawdust and slabs of wood from the mill. Old rusted equipment lay everywhere.

Tom took one look and said, "You'd think someone would clean up around here."

Ted and I were embarrassed and tried to get him to keep quiet, but he needed to be heard… more than once.

Beside the dock were the marine ways for hauling out boats for repair. Further back and to the left was the former hanger which was now the marine repair shop with the office at one end. A gravel road ran from the front of the office up the hill to the school.

Behind the office was a steep trail up to our house. The children called it the goat trail with good reason. You needed to hold onto roots and rocks to pull yourself, panting, to the top of the hill. It was weeks before I found out there was an easier way to get up the incline.

On the first day we arrived, everyone wanted to inspect the new teacher and to meet this new family. There were only about thirty people in the camp and new arrivals were an event. I was invited to a home for coffee almost as soon as we arrived. I have never seen such a dirty house in my life. I wondered where to sit down. Even the front of the refrigerator was covered with something thick, brown and anonymous. I'm not sure what it was but it ran in streams and then congealed. Worse of all was the coffee cup which had a similar surface. I tried to be polite, but it is hard to drink without touching any part of a cup.

Finding a suitable baby-sitter was a problem. Our first sitter was a young woman from Bella Bella. As I left for school in the morning of her first day at work, I told her we would be home for lunch just after twelve and would have pork and beans. When we arrived home, there were two tins of cold green beans open on the table, lids still half joined to the can, no dishes, and no silverware. When I questioned her, she indicated we could all help ourselves. She had never seen a table set for a meal. I taught her how to do this. She learned and seemed to take pride in setting the table correctly from then on.

As Anita did the housework, she had the radio blaring out popular music. Susan trailed behind her all day, dancing to the music. Susan did not really learn to walk, but only to dance.

After she had been with us for some time, she began to stay out late ay night, "jumping on". The girls from the village used this expression when they visited fishermen on their boats.

It was my habit to leave early for school after we had breakfast, and our sitter would help the children finish getting ready for school. One morning the children arrived with the remains of their breakfast on their faces and uncombed hair.

"Why didn't the sitter comb your hair?" I asked.

"She went back to bed," was their answer.

I immediately locked the school door, stormed up the hill to our house and routed her out of bed. Then I fired her.

The next evening her mother and brother came to see me. They demanded that I rehire her. Their family needed her income. She must come back to work for me. I would not be persuaded. The sitter was truly and definitely fired. Later I heard that her brother had just been released from prison where he served time for murdering his girl friend. Then I really felt my legs go wobbly.

Shearwater had been an air force base during WW II and Andy had bought the camp with all its facilities as war surplus. Besides the hanger, there were two H Huts each with living quarters for four families, a teacherage which we did not use as it was too small, a one-roomed school, two or three individual houses and a four-plex in which we lived.

This building had been the officer's housing and stood at the top of a small hill. Originally, it had been divided into separate rooms for the servicemen. When it was remodelled for family units, partitions were simply built to divide the building into four apartments. Each had a long hallway with identical rooms off each side.

We had a kitchen, four bedrooms, a living room, a bathroom, a laundry room, and a furnace room.

The kitchen was large and had many cupboards. In one corner was an oil range. An oil tank was supported on a metal frame outside the kitchen window. The oil was fed from the tank through a copper tube into the range. When the tank was empty, the truck from the office came around and refilled it. This was an efficient cooking system if we did not run out of oil, get water in the fuel or get "sooted up". I know about each of these eventualities.

The worst was if the stove became sooted up. It did not seem, at first, to be burning as hot as usual. Suspicion would enter my mind. Soon there was no doubt as I opened the lid and barely any flame was evident. Huge festoons of carbon filled the fuel box.

Special tools were provided to clean the stove. I removed all the cover plates because the soot filled the area under the entire stove surface. Step two involved scraping away all of these strings of carbon. Then, with another type of scraper, I scratched off the heavy carbon encasing the hot water pipes inside the box. A problem of what to do with this black mess was solved as I laid out newspapers on which to put the carbon. This worked fine unless someone opened the door to create a draft or walked near the stove. Finally, I replaced the lids and turned on the oil. When I saw exactly the right amount of oil flow from the tank, I threw a lighted match into this stream of oil. Often the match went out as it fell into the oil or beyond it. Sometimes too much oil flowed in and a small explosion occurred. Infrequently, it lit on the first try.

It seemed to take exactly a week for the stove to become sooted up. That explained why, each weekend as I saw the boat carrying Ted off to distance ports, I would note the ominous signs of the stove slowly cooling down. The whole stove cleaning procedure took about two hours when I included the time washing the floor and parts of the walls that inevitably were covered with this oily soot.

The children loved to watch me clean the oil range. Of course, they had many comments to make me feel happy to be having so much fun.

"You're sure lucky you know how to clean a stove, aren't you," David would say.

"I'll bet no one else knows how to do this," Karen would pipe up.

And worse of all "Can I help?"

At the far end of our apartment was the furnace room containing an enormous homemade furnace. It was designed to hold the four-foot lengths of slab wood which were otherwise mill waste. A door had been cut into the furnace room from the outside so the mill truck could dump loads of wood conveniently close to the furnace. It was our family's job to pile the wood in the furnace room. After all, it was our furnace.

It was not, however, our heat. It rose to the upstairs apartments keeping them warm and cozy. In the winter, I set the alarm for every two hours and would grope my way to the furnace room, struggle with the heavy doors and lift about a third of a cord of wood into the gaping maw of that furnace. I did not dare to close the drafts too much as the wood was green and needed a good fire under it to keep the logs burning.

Because so little heat came to our rooms, we had an oil heater in the living room. This had an oil tank attached to its side. It held about two gallons of oil which had to be taken from the large oil tank outside the kitchen, carried into the living room, and emptied

131

into the tank. As the container was so small, the fire usually went out during the night.

The camp had a generator for electrical power, which was turned off in the evening. We had coal oil lamps to use at night. This added a new learning experience. The glass chimneys had to be washed each day as they, too, sooted up with carbon. The wicks had to be trimmed so they would burn efficiently and the base of the lamp was filled with coal oil each day.

In the morning, the generator was turned on. I heard the electric motors grind as they all came on at the same time. I never needed to defrost the fridge as the ice melted every night when the power went off. In the morning, my first job was to wipe up the water on the floor.

It was one of the men's jobs to start the generator each day. I would meet him as he was coming back from the generating plant and I was going to school. He would always greet me with some kind of suggestive remark or lurid offer. I never gave him the satisfaction of acknowledging his remarks. One day he asked Ted if I understood what he was saying.

"Of course she does," Ted replied. "She just won't become involved in that kind of conversation."

One wing of the H Hut was used as a community hall. Each month one family was in charge of the social activities for the month. Our month was December as I already had the responsibility for the Christmas concert. Each month there were Bingo parties, dinners, dances, and similar events.

Once a month, the minister from Bella Bella held church services in the hall. All the children, some of the women, Ted and Uncle Andy attended. Usually, one of the nurses came to teach a lesson to the children. On one occasion, a nurse was teaching the children about saying grace to show our appreciation for our food.

"We say grace at our house," Arlene spoke up. "We always say grace at supper time," she added. Now the nurse was beginning to lose her train of thought.

Undaunted, Arlene continued, "Sometimes we say grace at lunchtime." Now the congregation was beginning to turn their heads and smile.

Finally, Arlene piped up even more loudly, "But we never say grace at breakfast time." By this time, everyone was laughing and the teacher completely lost whatever point there was to her lesson.

Auntie Jean did not drink and was opposed to liquor in the camp. However, this viewpoint did not affect the workers. On one occasion, the boys in the camp collected all the beer bottles they could find and piled them, unknown to Jean, in the hallway to her front door. There were probably fifty cases. The minister from Bella Bella arrived to make his pastoral visit and came to the front door which Jean never used. Imagine her horror when she opened the door and saw all the beer bottles. With aplomb, she pretended she could not see them there, and, kindly, the minister pretended he had not noticed them. As soon as the minister left, so did the bottles and they were never put there again.

On Saturday nights, there were usually movies in the Community Hall. Chairs were set up and either National Film Board films or Fourth String movies were shown. Many people from Bella Bella would bring their families in their fish boats to watch the shows. We were always amused to hear the native children yell out, "Kill the Indians," in the most exciting part of the cowboy movies. They always related to the hero.

The children had complete freedom in the camp. Most of the island was covered with muskeg, swamp and stunted evergreen trees. Around the buildings, however, sawdust from the mill was spread to keep weeds from taking over and to keep the roadways and school playground dry. There were gun emplacements and air raid shelters still on the base and these afforded interesting places in which to play. The air raid shelters were like huge cement culverts, open at both ends. The rainfall in this area was over 180 inches a year so the children were lucky to have shelter, but still fresh air in which to play.

David & Tom giving Susan a first bike ride

Getting clothes dry was a constant challenge. One day Ted came home for lunch and I was hanging out the clothes in a heavy rain.

"What in the world are you doing?" Ted questioned me.

"I'm hanging out the clothes because it is going to stop raining in a few minutes," I replied.

"Whatever makes you think that?" was Ted's response.

"In the Fraser Valley, as soon as the birds begin to fly during a shower, it immediately stops raining. The birds are now flying and I'm going to get my clothes dry outside today."

"If the birds here waited for the rain to stop before they flew out to get food they would all starve to death," Ted laughed.

I brought the clothes back in, rewrung them through the wringer, hung them on lines in the laundry room and waited for nearly a week for the next drying day. It was a sad lesson to learn that, in the north, not even the birds can be trusted to tell the truth.

Many squirrels lived in the woods close to our house. One, in particular, used to come to the boys' bedroom window and make scratching noises to indicate he wanted attention. Then the children would put peanut butter on their fingers and he would lick it off. He particularly liked Karen to feed him. I guess she was the quietest and most patient.

There were also many wolves on the island. At night, we could hear them quite close to our house. At one time, there was a family from Australia who lived in our building. The wife had heard many stories about wolves and how dangerous they were. She sent her husband out each night at bedtime to walk around the apartment building to make sure there was no wolf at her door. What could her husband have done if he had met the wolf, I wondered?

On another occasion, this same woman was helping Jean wash the bedding for the bunkhouse. It was heavy work and the next day her arms were very stiff and sore.

"What do you think I have?" she asked Jean, who was a nurse.

"Well," said Jean," I'm sure you have sheetitis."

Then panic took over. This woman really believed she had a serious medical condition. Though the rest of us in the camp tried to reassure her that her illness was not terminal, she wanted to go to Bella Bella for a complete medical examination to eliminate the most serious of her fears. She did survive!

Sometimes people from the camp would meet wolves on the road to BC Packers store, but the wolves always crept away. This road was partly gravelled, but was mostly a boardwalk built over the muskeg. It was about a two-mile hike to the store and often on Saturday, a group would go together to shop.

On Wednesday, each family sent a list of everything they would need for the next week: groceries, shoes, school supplies, or hardware to the marine office. The order went by boat to Bella Bella, to be filled when the freighter arrived on Thursday morning. The company boat delivered the orders to Shearwater. Then the orders were off-loaded to the company truck, which delivered the supplies to each house.

We looked forward to getting mail once a week and especially the Vancouver Sun newspaper. I tried to ration myself to one paper a day, even though it was more than a week old by this time. Radio reception was poor as we only got one station in the evening and no reception most days. Somehow, what went on in the outside world did not seem very important.

Many mail deliveries also brought us parcels from the T.Eaton Company or Simpson Sears mail order catalogues. The children eagerly looked forward to the arrival of the Christmas Wish Book as it held treasures undreamed of from the BC Packers store. Each child marked a large number of items desired for Christmas and hoped Santa would bring them.

When asked what they wanted for Christmas, they would answer something like, "I want item # 4593 on page 12 in blue (option 06)"

Each had memorized every detail of their desires. Such was their faith that usually Santa got it right.

Every Christmas, Andy took the Lady Marjory to Ocean Falls for Christmas shopping. Earlier the men went out and cut Christmas trees which were loaded on the deck of the boat and sold in the "city". There was one store owned by the Hudson Bay Company, filled with items too numerous for the children to even imagine. Many children had never been out of Shearwater and thought Ocean Falls was like fairyland. We also took our baby-sitter with us the first time we went to Ocean Falls. Coming from Bella Bella, she had never seen anything like the store, restaurant, Christmas lights on houses, or a real theatre and bowling alley. She talked of nothing else for months.

The school was the centre of the children's lives. All activities revolved around school projects. There was no outside entertainment except the occasional movie.

The school building consisted of two large rooms. One was the classroom and the second an activity room where we had our PE classes and where the children played at recess. I had eleven students in grades one to eight. I also supervised correspondence classes for two boys who were in grades nine and ten. Actually, though I tried to group the students for ease in teaching, most of their work was individualized, as the children's abilities were so diverse.

Two of the children were seriously retarded. One had been in Grade One the year before I came to Shearwater. At the beginning of his second year in this grade, he could do virtually no schoolwork. But, worse than that, he was not toilet trained. I would watch him carefully and when I saw him squirming in a particular way, I would look at him, say his name and he would clutch himself and run off to the washroom. At the end of his second year in Grade One, he could print his name, knew a few words from the pre-primer and no longer wet his pants in class. The next year I assigned him to Grade Two and we began again to learn to print and to read the pre-primer.

The older children each had a younger child to help: to listen to them read, and to drill them in vocabulary or number facts. Diane, to her credit, used to work with the lowest student. Perhaps this helped her learn to deal with the Special Ed students she often taught in High School when she later became a teacher...

No time was wasted. Children understood what they were expected to do for each class and went from one task to the next without direction. There were always many extra fun projects to do when the student had finished his work. It kept me busy, trying to keep ahead of the students with enrichment projects, games and puzzles.

Some city schools had spirit duplicators for preparing student assignments, but there was not one in my school. Instead, I made jelly pads for duplicating worksheets and tests for my students. Six jellyroll pans were filled with unflavoured gelatine mixed with hot water. When the jelly set, my duplicator was ready for use.

I then wrote out the assignment on a sheet of paper with a hectograph pencil, a product especially for this purpose. This paper was placed, written side down, on the jelly pad, smoothed evenly with my hand to be sure that all the paper laid smoothly on the gelatine surface. Some of the ink then soaked into the jelly. Working quickly, I then placed newsprint paper onto the surface, rubbed it gently to be sure the copy would be clear where the ink transferred to the newsprint. About thirty copies could be made from each original, though, of course, each copy became increasingly lighter. The jelly pads then sat overnight while the ink sank into the jelly and were ready for the next day's use. Each day I made six worksheets for future classes. After several months, the jelly would develop holes or cracks, and I would have to replace the gelatine. I could never have imagined the ease of using photocopiers and computers as I did in later years.

One year the Grade 4 classes in the province were given a standardized arithmetic exam in which my four students all received above the 95th percentile.

We had brought several boxes of books with us and the whole community read them. Our house had more books than the school. Twice a year we received a huge box of about fifty books from the Provincial Travelling Library. This was a wonderful service to isolated schools. Every month we also received books from the Scholastic Book Club.

As a Social Studies project in an "Our Community" unit, we decided to do some cleanup in the camp. Andy sent a truck to pick up all the garbage, old boards and pieces of rusted machinery we had collected. Four truckloads went to the dump.

Another day we decided to beautify the schoolyard by planting flower gardens next to the school. This was not easy as the soil was mostly gravel and had not been worked for years. The School Inspector unexpectedly arrived while we were all outside working on the garden. He seemed pleased and joined us in our project.

May Day 1963

One of the first questions I was asked upon arriving in Shearwater was if I knew how to do the Maypole Dance and, fortunately, I had done this for many years as a child and remembered it well. Shearwater celebrated the May 24th holiday with children's sports and races, and a food booth. The culmination of the day was the traditional Maypole Dance. The camp owned a Maypole, stored in the hanger. For the event, it was repainted white and new coloured ribbons were purchased and attached to the top. Dancers held these coloured ribbons and danced around the pole in one direction, winding the ribbons to form a pattern. Then they danced in the opposite direction unwinding the ribbons. The final

139

pattern formed was a basket weave made by alternating the ribbons over and under each other. It was difficult to master well.

I knew that two of my students could never do these manoeuvres so I convinced them that standing on the base of the pole and holding it securely was the most important part of the dance. Indeed it was, as the pole was very tall and could have toppled over if it were windy.

Now there were not enough dancers for the routine. Though they were only four and five years old, Karen and Arlene were conscripted to "come to school" and be part of the Maypole dancers. They did not have any trouble learning the patterns.

Arlene and Karen were inseparable. One day we were having a picnic on the tarmac. Karen leaned down in the water where the children were wading. Seeing something glistening in the water, she leaned over and pulled up two quarters. "Look what I've found," she called out.

"Now where is mine?" Arlene asked. Then she promptly pulled out two more quarters.

Despite how hard the other children searched, no more money was found. To Arlene and Karen, it was right and just that they should have exactly the same.

They insisted on dressing identically as well. I gave in to the extent that their dresses should be at least of different colours. They would have been happy to be indistinguishable. Most people thought they were twins and that is how they liked matters to be.

Each spring, Andy took all the schoolchildren on the Lady Marjory to compete in the Sports Day in Bella Bella village. We were very excited and decided we would make up some cheers to encourage our competitors.

Arlene & Karen

The cheers may have lacked something in originality, but we made up for this with enthusiasm.

One, two, three, four
Who are we for?
Shearwater, Shearwater
Yea! Yea! Yea!
    OR

Two, Four, Six, Eight
Who do we appreciate?
Shearwater, Shearwater
    Yea! Yea! Yea!

The people from the village just stared. Perhaps they had never seen cheerleaders before. Perhaps they were envious of our pompoms.

Several of the people in Bella Bella had turned their living rooms into small stores. Customers could dance to a record player, or buy candy, pop and other beverages. I went into one such store and asked for a cup of coffee. The storekeeper took me to a back room, set me down at a table by myself, took a special teacup from a top shelf, carefully wiped it off and poured me coffee which I drank in complete isolation. It was considered an honour to serve me. Teachers were held in high respect in the village at that time.

We had special friends from Bella Bella village, Dave and Kitty Carpenter. They owned the BCP 43, a seine boat fishing for BC Packers Fish Company. On one trip from Shearwater to Ocean Falls, Dave asked me if I would like to take the wheel.

As I took over, I said, "It's sure easier than driving a car. I don't have to watch the road."

Just then, I hit a huge log, partially submerged in the water. Fortunately, it did not do severe damage, but it was a good lesson for me.

Several years later, a rogue wave in Seymour Narrows hit the BCP43 and it sank to the bottom. The sea can be treacherous, even to experienced fishermen.

Ted and I were staying overnight in Martin Inn so asked Dave and Kitty if they would like to come to our room for a while. They refused because a rule stated that no natives be allowed in the hotel. Ted was furious. He insisted they join us. We could clearly see how frightened they were in the elevator, but nothing further came of the incident. It is shocking how much discrimination there was against native people. The Carpenters were community leaders, owned a large boat, and were in every way responsible citizens. Their treatment was a disgrace.

Shortly after this visit to Ocean Falls, the University of Hawaii invited Dave and Kitty to make a presentation of traditional native dancing to the university. The faculty were particularly interested in the similarities between the language of the Bella Bella natives and the Hawaiians. The vocabulary of the two groups was so similar that they could understand many words in each other's native language. There is a striking similarity, also, in the physical appearance of the two groups. Research has led credence to the belief by many of a common ancestry of the two groups.

Another highlight of the school year was the Christmas Concert. With such a variety of ages and levels of ability, it was difficult to select items for the programme that would include all the children. One year we produced "Hansel and Gretel" and the next year we did "The Three Billy Goats Gruff" as the main part of the entertainment. These plays involved elaborate costumes and sets. Short skits, action songs and carols filled the evening. Then Santa Claus came with treats and gifts. The children knew it was the real Santa that visited them, as there was no other Santa seen in the community.

During the spring of 1962, the cannery at Namu, which was used for the processing of herring, burned to the ground. The site needed to be cleaned up, the burned and rotting herring removed and the enormous metal storage tanks relocated. Andy got the contract for this job and Ted went with him to Namu to operate a bulldozer for the project.

Ted suggested that the family join him at Namu for the summer. There was a float house tied up at the dock we could rent.

"It will be fun," he added.

"Give me a week to think about it," I replied.

When Ted came home the next weekend I agreed I would go but only if I could take my washing machine.

As soon as school was out in June we loaded what we needed on the WL2, a landing barge used in WWII, and set off for our adventure.

Ironically, the name of the float house was the "Deluxe". The "Derelict" would have been more appropriate. At the prow was a kitchen, then a step down took you to a bedroom, a further step down to a second bedroom, and finally even further down was the bathroom. Because the lowest area was unheated, the floorboards in the bathroom were rotting. A piece of plywood was nailed around the toilet, but it, too, was largely rotted through so that when you sat on the toilet, you could feel the flooring begin to give way.

When we first arrived, the bedsteads were sitting with each leg on a wooden Coca Cola case. I soon put these boxes out on the deck. When it rained, I discovered their purpose. Water flowed in through holes drilled in the walls under the windows, swept across the floor and out holes drilled on the opposite side of the room. I had to retrieve the boxes after the first rain and return them to their true purpose.

The first morning we arrived Ted arranged for the camp electrician and plumber to hook up the power and connect a waterline to the float house.

When he came home for lunch, I exploded. "I am not going to wash the dishes in the toilet."

The hot water was connected to the bathroom and not the kitchen. That soon changed.

The houseboat was on huge logs so it could be towed as a raft. When the tide went out, it sat on the beach at a radical angle. I learned soon that my washing machine would not operate unless it was level. For this reason, I had a tide book in the kitchen so I could calculate when the boat would be level enough to do the day's washing.

In the morning, I would get all the children dressed, and then they put on their life jackets for the day. There was a narrow deck around the houseboat where the children played. Logs were tied to make a shallow enclosure around the boat. There was a rowboat in about the same condition as the Deluxe, which our children could use. It had several leaks so while Tom rowed, everyone else bailed. I even went for several rides, sitting in the bottom of the boat, with a wet bottom, mine that is.

Karen, Diane, Tom, Arlene
Namu – 1962

In the afternoon, we went up to the playground near the school. I would carry the two smallest, one under each arm, over the slippery logs which supported the boat, and up the trail to the road. One day I slipped on the logs and fell in between them. Fortunately, I was able to put both children safely onto the logs, but I could not get up. As the men were just going to coffee break, I yelled at them to come and help me but they must have thought I was just being friendly as they waved, called back and kept on going. Eventually, I was able to get up on the slimy logs and continue to the top with my cargo.

On another occasion, a friend of Ted's took me fishing in his outboard motor boat. We were trolling slowly, anxious to catch a salmon, and not paying particular attention to where we were going. Suddenly, we heard angry yelling, and realized we had trolled into the centre of a purse seine net which the crew was trying to close. No wonder the men were swearing at us. Despite this advantage, I did not catch a salmon and, in fact, have never caught a salmon.

Ted's job was to plan the method and then move the huge tanks which were used to store fish oil. From our window, we watched

145

him set up cables with an intricate system of pulleys and tackle to gain enough mechanical advantage to move the enormous weight with one small bulldozer. I have no idea where he learned to do this. He must have seen the technique when he worked in various logging camps.

One day one of the managers from BC Packers knocked at the door. I knew he was an official as he was wearing a suit and tie in a fishing village. When I saw him standing there, I recognized at once that something terrible must have happened to Ted. The thought that Ted was killed flashed through my mind. When the manager said that Ted had crushed his hand, I said, "Oh, is that all?" He must have thought I was a very uncaring wife.

A plane flew Ted to the Bella Bella Hospital. I quickly packed and the next day Andy Widsten took us home to Shearwater in the landing barge.

I was anxious to visit Ted in the hospital as soon as we arrived home. One of my students, Danny Trim, offered to take me in his motorboat. When we got as far as BC Packers, Danny suggested he would go into the store and get some candy to take to Ted. He said he would not tie up the boat, and I should just hold on to the dock for the few minutes he would be gone. I guess he was gone a little longer, because in a short while, I absentmindedly let go of the dock and the boat began to move slowly from the dock. Then I panicked.

I saw a man coming down the dock and I yelled, "Save me. I'm drifting out to sea."

He leaned over and with one hand gave the boat a little push back against the dock. I wondered why he gave me such a peculiar look.

The doctor tried to save Ted's finger, but it did not heal properly so after about two weeks it was amputated. While he was in the hospital, Ted told the doctor it would be a good time to have his hernia repaired, so this was done at the same time. Ted came home from the hospital just a few days before school was to start.

146

Our niece, Marilyn, from Quesnel, had just completed Grade 12 and was looking for work. It seemed an ideal arrangement for her to live with us and care for our children. We knew her well when she was younger and she was a kind and loving girl. She had been a good student and would be a positive asset to our family. David had gone to Vancouver in the summer to get new glasses (again) and he could return with Marilyn on the boat in time for school to open.

When Marilyn arrived at our house, she immediately barricaded herself in her bedroom and refused to come out. Later we learned she and David spent the entire trip north locked in their cabin.

By Sunday, Ted's patience had run out and he demanded she come out, which she did. Ted talked to her and she agreed she was ready to look after the children. She said she was stressed from her trip but would now be all right and ready to help the next day as school was beginning. We spent the rest of Sunday visiting with her and everything seemed fine.

Monday began normally. After supper, Marilyn went for a walk and did not come home. At first, Ted went out to look for her around the camp but he could not find her. When it began to get dark, the rest of the workers went out to search also. They searched around Coil Lake, the air raid shelters, and in all the obvious places, without success. Andy left the power plant running all night in case Marilyn needed a beacon to return safely. In the morning, Ted notified the police in Ocean Falls and their police boat was sent to Shearwater. Ted also chartered a plane to survey the island. There was still no sign of Marilyn.

As the children were going home for lunch the next day, a student ran back to the school to tell me he had found Marilyn. She was up in the rafters of an abandoned building curled up in a fetal position. Ted was immediately summoned and eventually was able to get her down out of the rafters.

David waiting to board the Lady Marjorie
En route to Vancouver, again

The police boat then took her to the hospital in Bella Bella. The doctor advised Ted she should be committed to the mental institution in Vancouver. The most difficult thing was to tell Ted's sister, Betty, what had happened to Marilyn. Betty was upset but not too surprised. She said Marilyn had been disturbed before she went north, but she thought we could help her regain her health. We had not known anything about her mental problems.

Despite the fact Ted was just recovering from a hernia operation and the amputation of his finger, he accompanied Marilyn to Vancouver on the next boat and signed all the papers to have Marilyn committed to a Mental Institution. He stayed in Vancouver for several weeks while he had physiotherapy for his hand.

I hired Rosie Hall, a woman about the same age as I. Although born in Bella Bella, she had lived most of her life away from the village. As a young child, Rosie had tuberculosis of the spine and was sent to Coquilitza, the hospital for native people, near

Chilliwack. For the entire fifteen years she was bedridden, she had no communication with her family during this time. Eventually, doctors decided she could learn to walk again, which she did with the help of a brace. Then Rosie was sent back to Bella Bella. It was not a happy time for her. Her father had remarried and had a second family, she could no longer enjoy the traditional Indian food, and she had forgotten the native language. Rosie felt she fit into neither the native society, nor the white culture.

Shortly after returning from Namu, I realized another baby was on its way. This was a complication as there were no substitute teachers in Shearwater. I wrote to the School Board, told them I was expecting another child at Easter time, and suggested I would keep the school open until I had the baby. Then we would have the usual ten days Easter-break. This they agreed to do. By this time, Ted had gone to work in Ocean Falls where we intended to join him as soon as school was completed in June. In case Ted was not home when the baby was due, he had arranged for Bob Gervan to take me to the hospital in his speedboat.

Easter came and went. On April 19, after school on Friday, a full week to the day later than planned, contractions began. We notified Bob, who by this time was having second thoughts about the speedboat. He and Bob Mathieson took me in the landing barge to Bella Bella. As contractions were every minute apart I was afraid the baby would be born in this dirty, oily workboat. But we got safely to Bella Bella only to discover the seine boats were in and we could not tie up to the dock. I had to walk across the deck of one boat, climb over the railing and across another boat and so on until I finally reached the dock. I was sure the baby would be born on the fish boat, or drop between the seiners. I could see the great sigh of relief from the two Bobs as the hospital pickup met us and their responsibilities were over.

Upon reaching the hospital, all contractions ceased and I just lay there talking to Dr. Chisholm for several hours. Then in one mighty push, Mary Ann Cecilia arrived. She weighed just over seven pounds and was very blonde. She was, we all agreed, a very beautiful baby.

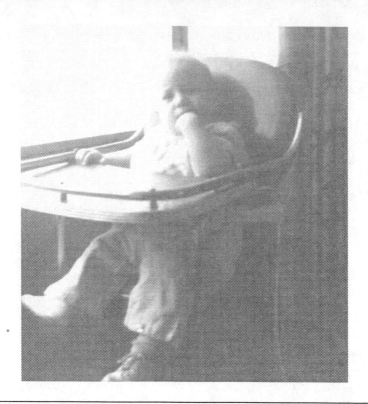

Mary Ann Cecilia – 4 months old

Ted had wanted each of our previous girls to be called Mary, but I thought Mary Brown was too plain a name. I finally relented if he would accept Mary Ann instead of just Mary. Then to make the name more distinctive, we added Cecilia, which was my Grandma McDonald's middle name. My Grandpa McDonald wrote and told me it was the best name we could have chosen because they were the names of the two women he loved the most, his mother and his wife.

When Mary Ann was a little older, she said very seriously. "Mother, I know I am not adopted as no one would adopt a seventh child."

The first night we brought Mary Ann home from the hospital, Ted and I played bridge with Hank and Ine Veelbehr who had recently moved to Shearwater from Vancouver. Hank was the new accountant for Andy. Mary Ann spent the whole evening sleeping on my knee. She was a wonderful baby, very easy to care

150

for. I am sure it was because she had eight parents. Her feet never touched the ground. One sound from her and everyone wanted to pick her up and play with her. As had been the case with Susan, each child wanted "to try her out". All my students also wanted their turns to hold her. No baby could have been more loved nor had more attention than she.

Shearwater Elementary: 1962-63
Back: Kevin, Nancy, David G. Angela, Joe, Diane
Middle: Robin, Harold, Tom, Brenda
Front: David B. Charles, David G.

Ocean Falls
1963-1968

T ed began to work as a town site electrician several months before the school term ended so was living in the Martin Inn in Ocean Falls. Because there was a severe housing shortage, the hotel arbitrarily assigned roommates. Ted's first companion was a young man who played a guitar. This was not a good arrangement as the guitarist wanted to play when Ted wanted to sleep. Later Ted shared a room with a congenial roommate, Brian Canfield.

George McKinnon wanted to sell his partially furnished house in Martin Valley. We had no money for a down payment, so Brian lent us the money as rent in advance for a room in our basement. This gave us the first home we owned and solved Brian's problem as to how he could get out of the hotel. There were now at least eleven people around our table for every meal - our family of seven children, Brian and Rosie. There were usually others as well, as the children often brought friends home for meals. Groceries were very expensive as freighters brought everything in from Vancouver. Although we both had well paying jobs, it took most of one income just to feed our family.

The house on Highland Drive was on the upper road overlooking the Martin Valley dock. From the front window, I could see the boats moored there. Despite my fears, the children rowed their skiff within a defined area marked by particular boom sticks. I never let on to them how worried I was as they were out rowing, but I kept a watchful eye from the front window. The children knew they had to wear their life jackets and they knew their freedom to row their boat would have been taken away from them if they had broken their trust with us. They never lost this privilege.

There were wooden plank roads in town with spaces between the boards through which the water drained when it rained, which it did almost every day. Often, as I walked in my high-heeled shoes I would catch the heel between the planks and have to stop, lift my foot out of my shoe, then yank the shoe free from the crack before going on. It was hard to feel sophisticated under these conditions.

Karen, David, Arlene
Susan, Diane, Mary Ann, Tom
Knitted suits made by Mother -- 1966

There was only about a mile of road from Martin Valley to town, but we soon found we needed a car to transport groceries in particular. Eventually a car came up for sale, a beige coloured Volkswagen beetle. Of course, it was too small for nine people but we managed to squeeze everyone in. There were no seatbelts then and no regulations about safety. Everyone was still small and flexible. I held Mary Ann on my knee in the front. Four sat on the back seat and two more crowded into the area behind the back seat, usually Karen and Arlene. Once we packed the groceries and schoolbooks into the remaining spaces, we were set to go. No one ever complained about being crowded. I guess it was better than tramping through the rain.

Ocean Falls
Town site on left, mill on right of dam

One October it rained day and night for the entire month. There was likely a rainfall record set, but we would never know as the rain gauges washed away. The rain came down so furiously during a winter storm, that it would hit the road and bounce back into my face so I could get soaked in two directions at once. Looking out of the windows at school it seemed as if someone were washing the windows with a high-pressure hose.

Although it seldom snowed, when it did, a frequent daily downpour of two inches of rain would become 20 inches of snow. In 1965 there was an extremely heavy snowfall followed by a southeasterly storm bringing warm weather and heavy rain. We were celebrating Susan's birthday when we became aware of flooding. The stream behind our house overflowed, causing water to fill our basement to a depth of several feet. A torrent flowed across the street and rushed like a river down the road and into the houses on the lower road.

A more serious tragedy happened in town. The rapidly melting snow caused an avalanche, which tore down the mountainside taking out several houses and damaging an apartment building. The slide that killed seven people cut off power to the Valley. A large landslide covered the road with debris. Communication to the outside world was severed.

Ted was working in the powerhouse and did not know if we were dead or alive. There was no way to find out. Eventually someone was able to get a boat from town to Martin Valley to check on the families there. For many days, a small boat went back and forth delivering groceries and taking people to work.

The Vancouver radio stations picked up the story, but did not have the correct facts. The first report stated, "Ocean Falls Wiped out by Huge Avalanche".

Our parents in the Fraser Valley were frantic. In a few days, telephone linemen restored, basic services but it was almost impossible to get a message. Ted's mother, who had lived in Ocean Falls for many years and knew the manager of the corporation when he was a little boy, finally got through to him.

"How is my boy, Teddy?" she asked.

In the midst of all the confusion, the manager was polite and gracious to her as he answered that he had not heard anything about Ted so he assumed he must be all right. We were embarrassed that she should have gone to upper management in her concern for her son, but could understand her worry.

The first year I was in Ocean Falls, I taught Grade Six. Again as the "new" teacher on staff, the principal assigned me to teach the lower division. I felt sorry for these students, as they had had at least two teachers each year since they began school. In that class, there were three sets of twins, an unusual occurrence. I found it a wonderful class, full of enthusiasm to learn and always very well behaved. I think they appreciated stability in their classroom.

The next year I began the year as a Grade Six teacher. However, in October, I transferred to the High School where I took over the Home Economics classroom. There was a severe shortage of teachers at that time, particularly in the elective courses. Many teachers taught with incomplete certification. I now began my years of summer school and correspondence courses to complete my university degree.

At first, I began to take Home Economics and Psychology courses with a view to becoming a High School counsellor. The requirement then was to be qualified in two teaching areas. Part way through completing these courses, the university removed Counselling from the list of teaching majors. I changed my second teaching major to Library.

The School Board had a policy to encourage the retention of teachers by paying their tuition fees for university courses if the teacher passed the course and returned to teach in Ocean Falls the following year. I took advantage of this opportunity. After each year of university was completed, I received an increase in pay. My salary was based on the number of years of university studies I completed, as well as the number of years I taught.

For several years, I was on the negotiating committee for the local Teacher's Association, one year as the chair of the bargaining team. This committee made a trip to Prince Rupert by boat and several trips to Bella Coola to work on negotiations. The year I was chair, we were unable to reach an agreement with the Board and we were forced into compulsory arbitration.

A group of arbitrators came from Vancouver to meet with the bargaining committee and the Board. They arrived by plane and expected to stay for a day or two, then fly back again to Vancouver. One of our requests was for an increase in the isolation bonus. We talked about how difficult it often was to get in or out of town, about delays in plane travel and other inconveniences. Nevertheless, the arbitrators would not accept this argument. They had not had trouble in their travel and felt we were exaggerating our request.

Charleson High School – circa 1940
Ted, Diane, Tom & David attended this school

After our negotiations were completed, we had a moose dinner at our house to wind up our meetings before they returned to Vancouver the next morning. Unfortunately, a storm came in, delaying any flights for two days. I often wondered if a storm had delayed their trip north to Ocean Falls instead of the return flight, if they would have been more sympathetic to our request for an increase in our isolation bonus.

Rosie Hall had come with us from Shearwater as our baby sitter, but after a few years, we felt we could manage without hiring anyone to live in our home. As Ted was now working shift work as a hydro operator in the power plant, one or both of us was usually home to care for Mary Ann and Susan. The older children were at school all day. Rosie went to live with our friend, Vic Robinson on his boat.

With our new arrangement to manage without a live-in housekeeper, Ted agreed that he could do the laundry when he was in charge of the house. The first day he spent in front of the wringer washer was the last day.

"I had no idea it took so long," he complained. "I spent most of the day down in the basement," he continued.

Susan, Arlene, Mary Ann
summer of 1963

I bit my tongue. I could have said, "I told you so." The next day we had an automatic washer and drier.

One day when I got home from work, Ted was very pale and distressed.

"Come into the bedroom," he said. "I have something to show you."

159

Walking over to the bed, I saw a gunshot hole through the gold coloured satin bedspread and into the mattress. Ted had been cleaning the gun and it had fired. It was a potentially dangerous accident and completely unexpected. Ted was experienced in handling weapons and always very careful in removing the shells and storing them away from the gun. For several years, we had the same bedspread with the glaring hole and the constant reminder about gun safety.

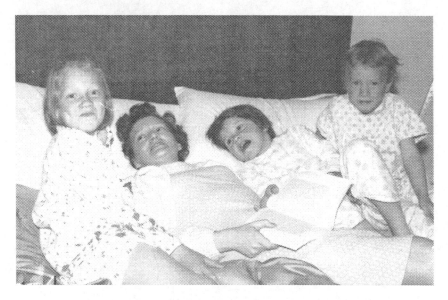

Arlene, Joyce, Susan & Mary Ann
Relaxing on the infamous bedspread

Often the only time Ted and I saw each other would be as the bus and our car passed on the road between work and school. For a short period, Mary Forbes looked after the girls, but although she was a nurse and had raised four children, she was not emotionally stable and we soon were looking for a different baby sitter.

We then found Kay Selzer who was a fanatical house cleaner. She could do more in one day than I could in a week. She particularly loved Susan and often took her to their cabin on Link Lake to play with her son who was about the same age. Many years after we knew Kay, I learned that her husband had killed her. What a sad ending to her life.

Bernice Colton asked me if she could look after my children. It was a perfect solution. No one could have been more kind and loving than she was. Each morning she came to the house when the older children left for school and did all my washing, ironing and mending. Then she took Mary Ann to her house for the rest of the day. This extra money was sufficient to send Bernice's son, Douglas, to school in Vancouver.

Diane, Karen, Grandma Pridmore, Arlene
Mary Ann, Susan -- 1966

We had several special visitors while we lived in Ocean Falls. A few months after we moved from Shearwater, I woke in the night to find my mother standing beside my bed. Without telling us, she had made the trip north on the boat, and then met people who had driven her from the boat to our house. What a wonderful treat it was to see her after two years. I think she was worried about

161

how we were doing so far from our family. She stayed with us for a few days before the boat returned for its trip south. I remember mother washing all the kitchen walls while she was visiting. I am sure that I never got all the finger marks off until the summer holidays.

Another visitor was Grandma Pridmore. We had a wonderful time as she played with all the children and shared family stories. She found it quite difficult to go up and down the gangplank of the steamship as she was about eighty years old.

When Grandma arrived she said, "It was the strangest thing on the boat. Almost everyone was carrying an umbrella."

I am sure she soon found out why this was true. We never, summer or winter, went out without an umbrella. Most years I would buy two or three as the wind would catch the umbrella and turn it inside out or tear the cloth from the frame.

In 1964, Ted's Mother and Dad came for a trip. Fred Brown had spent much of his life in Ocean Falls and the surrounding areas, but had not been back since he retired about twenty years before. He was so frail he could hardly walk off the boat. We were shocked to see how old and sick he seemed to be.

Fred Brown
Northland Prince arrives in Ocean Falls --1964

Ted arranged that we would take his parents on the Lady Marjory, captained and crewed by his old friends, Andy and Jean Widsten. We were gone several days exploring the old haunts that they knew so many years before. They reminisced about old friends they had known, those they had worked with in logging camps, and spent time with on hunting and fishing trips. By the time Grandpa and Grandma Brown went home, Grandpa was walking easily and seemed years younger. They had had a wonderful trip, as did we.

When they got home, they made a lengthy trip around BC visiting other family members and "old" Ocean Falls' people sharing news of their trip with everyone. Shortly after, on November 11, 1964, Fred Brown had a heart attack and died. Remembrance Day is always a particular day to think of Ted's Dad.

Later, Grandma Brown stayed for a summer when I went to UBC for six weeks. An exciting experience occurred when a young bear cub strolled into our back yard. Grandma was determined to get a picture, chasing him across several back yards before she took his picture for posterity. Grandma was lucky that the mother bear, which was surely near by, did not join in the mad chase.

Rhoda Brown's bear picture

In many ways Ocean Falls was well organized. There were many clubs and social groups. The children were involved in the Scouts and Girl Guides.

The town had a regulation Olympic sized pool with a qualified coach, George Gates. When Ted was in High School, he swam competitively and hoped our children would also desire to be swimmers. We soon enrolled them in swimming lessons.

Shortly after Susan learned to swim, there was a swim gala to raise money. Ted pledged twenty-five cents a length, thinking she would swim about ten lengths. However, she would not stop. Bravely she continued, 30, 35 lengths, her face flushed and her body obviously tired, but unwilling to give up. Eventually Ted had to pull her out of the water at 143 laps. I cannot imagine how long she would have lasted.

Ted and I played badminton often and frequently played bridge. Each noon hour the teachers played in the staff room. When we chaperoned at a school dance, the bridge table was set up near the dance floor. The dummy would get up, walk around the gymnasium, and then return in time for the next hand. There were few problems requiring teacher intervention.

Joyce with Santa (Colin Wright)

Christmas was a big social event. The Crown Zellerbach entertained the community with several cocktail parties in Company House. Teachers, nurses and their spouses went one night, office employees a second night and so on until each group was suitably entertained. The company hired a housekeeper to maintain the Company House and prepare food for out of town business leaders and for corporate entertaining. Guests dressed in the height of fashion for these lavish affairs.

The company also held a Christmas party for all the children of their employees. Each child received a generous gift from Santa Claus (The Company) as well as candy and other treats.

Another event eagerly looked forward to was "Willie Butner" night. A fellow teacher, Harry Higgins and his wife, Lois, lived across the road from a large rock on which was carved the message:

"Give to the world the best that you have and the best will come back to you".

Its carver, Willie Butner, signed it. No one knew who he was, or when he did the carving... However, a tradition grew up about Willie Butner. Each Christmas, the Higgins invited their friends to a party honouring the carver. Lois cooked massive amounts of food and made huge tubs of popcorn. The poets/guests arose in turn to toast the abilities of Willie Butner. As the evening progressed, Willie's accomplishments grew more improbable and sometimes even lewd, as the guests got deeper into the "spirit" of the party. Willie was given more talents than any man could ever have completed in a lifetime. Wherever you settled, Willie, there are people who cherish your memory.

October was Fire Protection Month and an occasion widely looked forward to by the children. For a small bundle of newspaper, a child could gain free admission to the theatre for an afternoon movie. It did not really matter if a child forgot to bring papers, as a friend would divide his piles. In the end, everyone was admitted.

The manager of the theatre, Reg Blackwell, became a good friend of ours and often came to our house for dinner. He died on a trip to Vancouver. As he wanted to be buried in Ocean Falls, his body was shipped north on a small floatplane. We attended the funeral service in the United Church, but before it began, the minister informed the congregation that only part of the funeral could be held that day. The body, which was to be transferred from one plane to another in Port Hardy, had inadvertently been left behind on the dock. Two days later, the casket arrived in Ocean Falls and we had the delayed burial. I think Reg would have appreciated the macabre humour in his funeral.

Somewhat later, Ted came to visit me while I was at Summer School in Vancouver. We decided to buy a new Volkswagen van and have it shipped north on the boat. As we were closing the deal, we asked the salesperson to put snow tires on it.

Joyce & Ted with the new van

"But it is August," he protested, "Shouldn't I have them put in the trunk for shipment?"

"I don't think you understand," Ted replied." We do not want regular tires. The wooden roads are too slippery for them. We use snow tires all year."

166

The sales representative just shook his head.

One summer we took all the family to Abbotsford for a holiday. First, a sling lifted the car onto the boat. We watched as a second car, swung into position for loading. Unfortunately, the sling did not hold and the new car crashed onto the deck, narrowly missing our car as there was no place to have car repairs done in Ocean Falls, the damaged vehicle continued on to Bella Coola, where a wrecker picked it up and towed it to a garage.

We then went over the Bella Coola road, a treacherous winding, narrow road going from one switchback to the next. We travelled fourteen miles in low gear. The children were not interested in the scenery or the historic facts I was trying to teach them as we moved over the Chilcotin plateau. They crouched down in the back of the van playing cards.

Everyone loved to play board games. Monopoly, Pit and Clue were favourites. Mary Ann loved to play Concentration, a game in which she turned all the cards face down, the tried to pick out two cards that made pairs. She seemed to do better than expected for a child her age, until we realized she had taken out all the nines and sixes that confused her.

David was our puzzle champion. He would time himself as to how quickly he could assemble jigsaws. He could visualize shapes, mentally rotate them, and then speedily see where each piece went.

Arlene and Karen loved to make craft items. They used every bit of cloth, ribbon or coloured paper; their imagination was a constant source of wonder to me.

These two were inseparable. When we first moved to Ocean Falls, Arlene was in Kindergarten and Karen in Grade One. Mrs. Dowling, Arlene's teacher, wanted to advance her to Grade One, but I refused to permit this, as I was afraid that, although Arlene could have easily done the work, it would have been unfair to Karen for her younger sister to be in the same class. Arlene was the only student who could tie her shoes at the beginning of the year so it became her special job to be the "shoe assistant" for Mrs. Dowling.

Arlene, David, Susan

Arlene, Karen
Rhoda Brown's, Surrey -- 1966

There were many blue jays in our back yard so David and Tom decided they would build a trap to catch them. The theory was that they would build a box with a string attached to the door. They put feed into the box and when the bird flew in to get the feed, one of them would quickly pull on the string and capture the bird. This project took several days of patience and hope. Many birds came close, but none was caught. There were, however, enough near misses to keep interest high. The novelty of holding the string for hours at a time waned and they eventually abandoned the project.

Unwittingly, Ted found a way to catch the birds. He had a recipe for making sake, a kind of Japanese beer made from rice and raisins. To these ingredients, Ted added sugar and yeast and allowed the mixture to ferment, forming alcohol.

When the brew was bottled, Ted threw the remains of the rice on the garden to rot down as compost, or so we thought.

Soon the jays began to arrive. They gobbled up the grain, and then wobbled around the yard. Soon more and more birds began to arrive as the word spread. Within hours, every grain had disappeared. All that remained were dozens of blue jays, all unsteady on their feet and easily caught by reaching out your hand. I do not think they would have cared if they were caught.

Ted instigated another project involving compost. He read in a magazine about the benefits and profits one could make raising earthworms. The principle was simple. You build raised beds from sheets of plywood and fill the beds with soil. To this, you add your kitchen scraps. Worms especially like coffee grounds and oatmeal porridge. "Just place the worms in the compost and nature will take care of the rest." stated the advertisements.

Soon the boys would be able to sell bait for all the local fishermen. Worm castings, a free bi-product, make an ideal fertilizer for houseplants. There might even be enough to supply the needs of those with flowerbeds. We certainly had all the required ingredients. Now we waited for the parcel containing the worms to arrive from Plains, Georgia.

In due time they came and the beds were ready to go into production. After a few days, we poked around and there did not appear to be too many worms. They were likely too small to see, since they had just hatched, we rationalized. (Do worms hatch?)

Then we noticed there were quite a few worms on the sidewalk, but we expected this after a rain. Eventually, we recognized that all the worms had migrated out of the beds and our dreamed of profits had done the same.

Tom, Rhoda Brown, David -- 1966

The owner of the business who sold us the worms did better. Jimmy Carter from Plains, Georgia, became president of the United States and later won the Nobel Peace Prize. Nevertheless, you will note, though he did not make his name in worms, they did give him a start.

Diane was always like another mother to her brothers and sisters. She assumed more responsibility than a young girl should have.

170

Diane began cooking dinner every night when she was in Grade Eight. Desserts and bread were her specialities. Diane learned to sew and made most of her own clothes. It is no wonder she later became a Home Economics teacher.

For many years, it had been Ted's dream to become a commercial fisherman. He was not happy working in the power plant. He found it depressing to sit listening to the turbines eight hours a day with no company and really nothing to do unless there was a breakdown.

When the opportunity came to purchase a gillnetter, he seized the chance. The Venture was in Vancouver so he flew there to bring the boat home. Although he had worked on the tug in Mount Lehman and on the barge in Shearwater, he had never made such a long trip up the coast and across the Sound alone. Ted had no radio on the boat so we just waited for him to come into port.

Venture

It was exam time. David was writing his Grade 7 math test; but his mind focused on the boat expected to arrive that day. From time to time, he would get up to sharpen his pencil and look out into the channel to see if the boat was in sight. On one such foray, he spotted the boat, handed in his incomplete exam and raced down to the dock to be the first one of the children to see the new boat. Ted had some scary moments on his trip north, but we were all glad to see him arrive safely.

Now the next chapter in our adventurous life was about to begin.

Joyce, the "Unsinkable Molly Brown" & Ted

Bella Coola
1968-1969

After school was out in June, we loaded our furniture on one of Andy Widsten's scows and he towed it to Bella Coola.

We bought the original Widsten farmhouse on five acres of land almost across the road from Andy and Jean's house. The Widstens were part of a large group of pioneers who had come to the Bella Coola valley from Minnesota in around 1890.

There were only two groups in the valley, the native people and the pioneers' descendents. The other residents were considered outsiders even if they had lived in the valley for many years. We did not seem to get that label, possibly because the Browns had lived in logging camps in the area since 1916 and knew many of the pioneer families. Because Bella Coola had been isolated for many years, it tended to be quite insular.

One year before Fred Brown retired he and Ted's brother, George, went by bicycle from Bella Coola over the summit to the Anaheim. The road then was no more than a trail. It was an adventure of a lifetime. In 1968, it was still an adventure.

A few years before we came to the valley, Andy and some other men from the community, bulldozed a road from Bella Coola up the mountain to access the road through the Anaheim plateau to Williams Lake. Although the road had been improved over time, it still required the car driver to go fourteen miles in low gear to get to the summit. From the passenger's window, one could see several switch backs below and the river, like a crayon line at the bottom. There were few places for cars to pass so if two cars met, one would have to back up. This was frightening as there were no barricades at the edge of the road.

Eventually the road was improved so that trucks and buses could make the trip. For many years, if a tourist with a camper-trailer unit wanted to visit Bella Coola by road, he must leave the camper at the summit and drive downhill with only the truck, as the unit was too long to make the sharp curves on the road.

The Widsten farmhouse had been vacant for some time so it required a thorough cleaning. Upstairs there was a large storage space under the eaves that was full of all kinds of interesting things, mostly junk, but exciting for the children to discover. The parts of the walls that were exposed showed the insulation- old newspapers with turn of the century advertisements. We could have wished for better insulation than newspaper, when the temperature dropped to -20 degrees.

One of my first jobs was to light the oil range to get hot water for cleaning. With a roar, the fire took off. In no time, the whole range was literally red hot. I was afraid the house was going to burn down. I immediately shut off the fuel supply and the stove eventually cooled down. 'Luckily' I knew how to rebuild the carburetor.

An early problem was with the water pump, which was not working properly. I had no one to help as Ted was fishing, so I decided I would have to repair it myself. I had no idea what to do, but bravely took it apart, examined the pieces and realized it was not too complicated a piece of machinery. I then reassembled it and, like a miracle, I primed the pump and got water. I hated to think a mere piece of equipment was smarter than I was.

The winter we spent in Bella Coola was the coldest since 1894. The winds blasted in from the Chilcotin like a funnel down the valley. Preceding the cold, we had heavy snow. Several feet filled our long driveway. Ted and the two boys shovelled it out so we could get to school. Inside the house, we could hardly keep warm with the oil range and a wood heater in the living room. We had a forest of birch trees on the property and it became a massive job to keep wood cut to stoke the heater with its insatiable appetite. There was a grill above the heater to warm the upstairs bedrooms. The coldest room in the house was the bathroom. Condensation froze on the walls so they were always covered with hoar frost.

Worst of all, in the middle of this freeze up, our well went dry. Cove McDowell, a fishing friend of Ted's, had come to live with us during the winter lay-off. He was stationed in Korea during the war and had seen how the Korean peasants drilled wells.

Karen dressed for winter fun
1968

First, a huge fire pile was ignited to thaw the ground at the well location. A tripod was erected with a pulley and a pail on a rope to carry up the soil as it was dug out of the well. One person was in the well digging, while others on the top hauled away the soil. It was cold, back breaking work, but eventually water was reached and the well was cribbed and covered.

Next door lived the Clarence Hall family. They had about the same number of children as we did and of approximately the same ages. The Halls built a long toboggan slide behind their house which they lit with several strings of Christmas tree lights. It was a great gathering place for the neighbourhood.

The freezing conditions made driving hazardous at times. One day as I was driving home from school, the road was covered with a sheet of ice. I was an inexperienced driver and had never driven in less than ideal conditions. Suddenly the car went faster and faster even when I took my foot off the gas. I did not know what to do as I careened down the road. At last, I saw Trepanier's driveway with no one on it. I turned the wheel as hard as I could and came to a stop with the nose of the car in a snow bank at the edge of the driveway. I found out later the gas pedal had frozen.

The next day one of our children's friends said, "Your Mother is sure a good driver. We saw her going really fast down the road when it was covered with ice." Little did he know what was going on at the time.

I had another frightening experience driving in Bella Coola. Shortly after we arrived there, Herb Quast, my driving instructor and the Forestry Officer for the area, took us to pick pinecones. Particular trees were identified as having cones suitable for tree planting. It can be profitable to gather the cones for sale. Never a family to turn down an opportunity for financial gain, I loaded everyone with a pile of burlap sacks into our van. Herb's family followed us up a steep, winding mountain road to make our fortune.

Perhaps some other family had reached the "good" trees before we got there, because we found no pinecones of any value. Coming down the narrow mountain road, I lost control of the car. I could not seem to remember what to do with the gears. Or, was it the brakes that confused me? I know now, though, that you should not go into this kind of situation when you have just received your driver's license. Eventually we found a convenient place to stop the van and Herb got his car in front of ours and guided me safely off the mountain.

A new philosophy in education was the concept of the open area classroom. There were no walls within the school. Teachers would plan and work cooperatively and children could be grouped together for one subject then regrouped for another depending on their levels of ability. It was in some ways an extension of the one-roomed school.

Mary Ann, Susan, Karen, David

The Elementary School in Hagensborg was one of the first in the province to be built especially for this purpose. I was excited to be appointed as the Grade Four teacher in this new school.

No one else on staff, however, was pleased to be a part of this new concept. There was no joint planning and very little cooperation. The first day of classes found the teachers looking around for cupboards, desks, anything to create some kind of walls. Each teacher stayed in her own territory as if the walls were actually there. The only difference was you could now hear everything going on in the other classes.

I was next door to a screamer. The first time I heard a huge bellow from across the "hall" I jumped.

177

"Oh, that's just the Grade Two teacher. You'll get used to it," my students said. However, I never did.

I also never got used to the very rigid and authoritative way the teachers handled their students. I felt sorry for the constant punishment and criticism that was meted out to them. It was not a happy environment. Within my own class, however, I really enjoyed my students. They were eager to learn and we had a good time together.

On one occasion, I took my class to visit the famous petroglyphs between Hagensborg and Bella Coola. They are renowned because this was one of the sites visited by Thor Heyerdahl, author of "Kon-Tiki", and described in one of his books. A large natural amphitheatre arose above a small creek. High on the cliffs surrounding it could be seen the ancient carvings which apparently pre-dated the stories of the local natives. The meanings of the pictures have never been deciphered. The local Indians told a creation story of the Great Flood similar to that related in the Bible. The local version states that only the top of one mountain remained uncovered.

Another favourite place to swim and picnic was the Beaver Pond on Andy's property. We also liked to explore and picnic on the Bella Coola River bank.

Diane, Tom and David were all in High School which was next door to the elementary school. Susan, Arlene and Karen were in the same school as I and Mary Ann went to kindergarten at Ine Veelbehr's home.

One day Mary Ann came home and told us it was Ine's birthday that day. We did not know this, but raced off to the store to buy her a gift. That evening we took it with some special refreshments to Ine's to honour her birthday. It was indeed a surprise party as it was not her birthday. No one knew how Mary Ann got that idea. Even from a young age, she always looked for an opportunity to have a party.

Tom, Arlene, Quast girls, David
Fun on the bank of the Bella Coola River

Television arrived in Bella Coola in 1968. It was installed at school and we often watched the school broadcasts, special programmes developed by the Department of Education, to fit the curriculum. Few students had television at home so the programmes were very popular.

Reception was poor because of the surrounding mountains. Our television set at home had "rabbit ears", a type of aerial that sat on the top of the TV and helped to bring in the programmes. Wrapping the antenna with aluminum foil also helped improve the reception. By accident, we discovered that if someone stood by the TV and held onto the antenna, the reception would be even better. It then became the job of the children to take turns holding the rabbit ears so all could enjoy the programmes. No one seemed to object to this task.

One day Karen had a sliver and went upstairs to get a needle to remove it. Coming downstairs, she dropped it on the floor. Quickly she said, "Well, at least it is stairilized" Karen had a good vocabulary and was creative in expressing herself.

Back: Tom, Arlene Jean & Andy Widsten, Rhoda Brown
Front: Susan, Karen, Mary Ann, David

We bought Mary Ann a slinky for Christmas. Before it was wrapped, Tom tried it out. He was fascinated by it and as soon as Mary Ann went off to bed, he would try it on the stairs. Eventually he wore it completely out and Mary Ann never did receive it as a gift.

We were invited to Ine and Hank Veelbehr's for Christmas dinner. Cove had gone out in his boat a few days before Christmas and we had not heard from him though we did expect him for Christmas dinner. The day before Christmas a heavy storm came up and intensified on Christmas day. There would be little chance for a small boat such as Cove's to survive. Andy and Ted went out on the Lady Marjory in particularly heavy seas to look for Cove's boat. They eventually found the boat, floating with a blanket as a sail, and brought Cove safely back to land in time for a delayed Christmas dinner. Cove did not say much, but was grateful his life had been saved.

Cove McDowell, Cove's friend, Ted

Cove had been separated from his family for many years and they had lost contact with him. One day I received a phone call from his mother in Ontario. She had never given up hope of finding her son and somehow had traced him to our address. From that time, we talked frequently on the phone and eventually Cove communicated with his parents.

Later his parents moved to Ocean Falls to be with him. Some time after that, his wife and children were also reconciled. He told me that living with us that year in Bella Coola had made him think of his own family and to foster the hope they might be reunited.

We had moved to Bella Coola because it seemed a better base for Ted's fishing, but in fact, he was away even more than when he was in Ocean Falls. We also realized that the High School was not as academically challenging as the one in Ocean Falls. Though I really enjoyed my Grade Four class, the open concept was doomed to failure. We decided to return to Ocean Falls the next year. My former Home Economics position was open and we resumed our life much as if we had never been away.

181

Back to Ocean Falls
1969-1974

A fter a year in Bella Coola, we returned to Ocean Falls. We bought a house on Garden Drive which had the identical floor plan to the house we had formerly owned on Highland Drive. It had hardwood floors throughout and the basement was completely finished with a self-contained suite. We needed all the space for our family.

David & Tom playing basketball
Back yard on Garden Drive

From the boys' room downstairs, was a patio door out to the garden area. There was a large terraced lawn sloping to the Martin

River which ran at the edge of our lot. The yard had been beautifully landscaped with two cement ponds which emptied one into the other. On the edge of one pond sat a statue of a little Negro boy casting his fishing line into the water. Just one lot away, the river emptied into the ocean. In the fall, the salmon migrated up the Martin River to spawn. Often we saw eagles swooping down to catch their dinner. At other times, we saw bear fishing for the unsuspecting salmon.

Mary Ann & Arlene

We were appreciative of the school system in Ocean Falls which was much better organized and more challenging than that in Bella Coola.

We soon settled back to our life, and in a short period, it hardly seemed we had been away. Diane was now in Grade twelve and preparing to go to university.

Graduation was a huge event in Ocean Falls, if not in numbers at least in the planning, money raising events and general excitement. Diane made her graduation dress as her Home Economics project. All the girls traditionally wore white dresses and the boys rented white tuxedos.

Karen, Diane, Arlene
Mary Ann Susan -- June 1970

The teachers marched in at the beginning of the ceremony dressed in academic gowns. Well, actually they were choir gowns borrowed from the United Church. Then the students followed. They had previously been to a dinner at the Martin Inn Hotel dining room.

The Home Economics department was always very involved in graduation. We measured and sent orders for the tuxedos to Vancouver. Before the ceremony, we practiced with the girls how to walk gracefully up to the stage with high heels and a long dress. Finally, we set the tables in the Lab and practiced how to behave at a formal dinner.

"Don't sit down before the hostess." That would have been Helen Moore, the principal's wife.

"Break off and butter a small piece of your bun at a time."

"Place your napkin beside your plate when you finish your dinner," and all the other niceties of an elegant meal were taught.

Many of the students were afraid they would do something wrong and embarrass themselves on such a special occasion, and really tried to be as well mannered as possible.

The graduation dance was preceded by the Grand March. Students walked around the gymnasium so all their parents and guests could admire the girls' beautiful dresses. They beamed in pride as their children marked this turning point in their lives. For many families, this student was the first person who had ever completed high school.

Following the ceremonies, the Home Ec classes prepared a reception for about two hundred guests. Fancy sandwiches, tea dainties and punch were served. Just before the ceremony was over, I would leave the gym with a team of student helpers to serve the refreshments.

One year when I arrived to our serving area, I found a panic situation. While we were in the gym, a table holding the huge urns of punch had collapsed spreading gallons of sticky punch over an enormous expanse. With mops and towels, the girls tried to get up the mess and make more punch before our guests arrived. We did not say anything about our disaster as we served, but some people must have wondered why their feet kept sticking to the floor.

It was always a relief to have a break from school at Christmas time. The day after the Christmas dance in 1969, I woke early with the thought in my mind, "The school burned down last night."

Imagine my surprise to get a telephone call shortly after this to say that not only the High School, but also the Elementary School had

186

been destroyed by fire. It had started in one building and quickly spread across the wooden road that separated the two buildings. Nothing was saved. The police believed it was caused by an arsonist as several aerosol tins were found in the charred remains of the school.

Investigators were called into the town and many students and teachers were interrogated. Some were asked to take a polygraph test. I wanted to take this test as I thought it would be very interesting, but no one considered I was even worth questioning. Although the police had several suspects, I do not think anyone was ever charged with the crime.

School site – taken from 10th Street looking down

By the end of the Christmas vacation, arrangements were made for the housing of all classes and we did not miss a single day of school. The elementary school relocated to the Community Hall and the High School took over one floor of the Martin Inn Hotel. Walls were taken down between three bedrooms, making them into one classroom. The sinks and bathtubs were left in the

187

classrooms. In the library, one bathtub became the "shelf" for the set of encyclopaedias.

For the first few months, I held my Home Ec. classes in a large room next to the cafeteria. We had acquired several sewing machines and a number of banquet tables. Every class became a textiles class. After a few months, we moved upstairs with the rest of the school.

I held my Foods classes in one of the modified rooms. An open set of shelves held our dishes, cutlery and one set of pans. We had large plastic garbage cans in which to do the dishes. Students used a saucepan to empty water from the small bedroom sinks into the garbage cans. Two electric ranges removed from vacant apartments were wired into the former bedrooms.

Joyce in the foods room

Having High School in an operating hotel created several problems. If a senior student was missing class, one of the teachers would have to go down to either the pool hall or the beer parlour and return the student to class. Somehow, everyone pulled together and we completed the school year.

As a Home Economics teacher, I liked to keep up with the fashion trends. In 1969, "stay-ups" came on the market for the first time. Previously women wore stockings, which were held up with a garter belt. This belt had attached to it, 2 grippers on the front and back which held the stockings in place. As you walked, the belt would move about on your waist, causing the stockings to go out of alignment. Nylon stockings had a seam, which was supposed to go straight up the back of your leg. They never did, but instead would turn and twist, so visually you looked either bowlegged or knock- kneed, sometimes both at the same time. I was always trying to twist my garter belt back in place either to straighten my seam lines, or to remove the garter belt from my crotch.

Foods class in the hotel

Stay-ups had elastic in the top and, never again, would I need to wear a garter belt, claimed the advertisers. The stockings, in theory, would sit snugly just above the knees and never be out of alignment. I think they were designed for women with fatter legs than mine. I was standing up in front of my class one day, when I felt a slight shiver just above my knee. A similar movement above my other knee followed this. I realized shortly, as the strange feeling continued, that my marvellous new fashion convenience was letting me down, and their ominous movement was accelerating with each shudder. Soon they would reach below the

189

hem of my skirt where my legs were even thinner and drop precipitously fast. I would be truly embarrassed.

Gliding as smoothly as possible to keep the impending disaster at bay, I eased toward the door and escaped quickly into the elevator where I was able to take my stockings off on the way down, and hide them in my pocket on the way back up. No student remarked that I had bare legs. Back to the garter belt until pantyhose came on the market.

During the building of the High School, many boys including Tom and David were hired to work on the steel beams above the gymnasium ceiling. I wonder now how they ever were allowed to do such dangerous work. The boys pointed out to the contractors that these huge beams were not properly bolted together, but their words were ignored. What could teenagers know about building?

The school had a huge library at the centre of the building with classrooms, or pods as the new terminology named them, opening off the research centre. The library included a lounge area for the students with comfortable chairs and chesterfields. The Home Economics Lab had six kitchens, which I helped to plan, complete with an automatic washer and dryer. It was a perfect area in which to work.

Besides the Industrial Education, area there was an enormous gymnasium. It was designed to be a community gym which meant it was larger than our school enrolment qualified for. A curtain could divide the gym into two basketball courts so that two classes could have PE at the same time. During the day, the gym belonged to the school; at night and on weekends, the community controlled the gym activities.

To celebrate the official opening of the new school, many dignitaries came to Ocean Falls from the Department of Education. Tom, who was the president of the Student Council at the time, was invited to the official dinner for these guests. The Minister of Education asked Tom what his plans were after High School. Tom told him he was planning to go to university.

The minister said words to the effect, "After the first year you will drop out. You should consider taking a trade."

190

It seemed the Department of Education had little confidence that students from a small rural school could succeed.

That winter we had an extremely heavy snowfall. Several times Ted, with Tom and David, shovelled many feet of snow off the roof of our house. Because the snow is extremely heavy on the coast, the weight may cause a roof to capsize. In fact, several did in the valley. Thus, the boys had a profitable job clearing off roofs. The snow piled up several feet in front of our house until some cars were completely buried in snow. There finally was no place to put any more snow. It looked as if our Volkswagen van was in a tunnel.

One winter day I arrived at school about 7:30, as was my custom. Frank Moore, the principal, arrived at the same time. The ceiling of the gymnasium had just collapsed from the weight of the snow. Many classrooms were also extensively damaged, not only by the collapsing roof, but also by the water damage which occurred at the same time as the heavy snow poured into the building and subsequently melted. There was debris scattered everywhere on the sidewalk in front of the school. The dust had not even settled so the accident must have occurred just seconds before we arrived.

Frank and I acted without thought. No one had yet arrived so we went together into the office and grabbed all the most important records we could carry. By the time we went out with this first load of documents, the fire department came along and prevented us from entering again. Fortunately, there was no one else in the school. Half an hour later the gym would have been full of students playing basketball before school started. Many lives would have been lost. The boys' question about the bolting of the beams seemed prophetic.

Destruction of the gym

One day soon after, the mill announced that it was closing permanently. There had been no warnings and the town was completely stunned. Many workers had never had another job except in Ocean Falls. Some workers transferred to other mills throughout BC, but most had no training for any other type of work and few prospects.

Canada Manpower, a government agency, came to town to set up appointments to explain what kinds of grants were available to pay for family's transportation and for the moving of their furniture to a new location. As the town was closing, it was not only the company employees who were affected, but also all the service employees, and the school, hospital and police force members who would have to relocate.

When it was my appointment time, the officer said to me, "Mrs. Brown, you do not qualify for a relocation package. Your husband does not qualify, as he does not work for the mill or any of the government agencies. You are not the head of your household, so you do not qualify either."

192

"Do you mean," I said, "that we will be the only family in Ocean Falls whose moving expenses will not be paid by the government?" Actually, there was one other family, John and Millie Fair, who owned a small radio business, who also were not eligible.

Then I said coldly, "There is only one thing I can do. I will divorce my husband. I will then be the head of my family and my expenses will be paid."

I did not raise my voice, but spoke softly and slowly as I have found this is the best way to get someone's attention. I then left the room.

The next month when Canada Manpower returned to Ocean Falls, I received a phone call to come to their office. When I arrived, the agent told me, "Mrs. Brown, we have reconsidered our policy. Your family will be eligible for the same compensation as any other family."

However, in the meantime, the BC government bought the mill and town site and the mill continued to operate. Many of the best-qualified workers along with many of our best academic students had already found jobs in other places and did not want to change their plans. I had accepted a teaching position in Houston, but was allowed to stay in Ocean Falls because the superintendent covered both areas.

Many workers who were on welfare in the Maritimes were hired to come to Ocean Falls. The students, overall, were academically much lower than our students. A new academic bottom was created. Those students we formerly considered low in achievement, now appeared to be not so bad in comparison.

All the students worked in the mill on weekends and holidays as soon as they reached 16 years of age. Their wages were very high. Students earned more sweeping the washrooms on the weekends than did beginning teachers with five years of university training. No wonder some students did not see any reason to complete school.

Diane worked in the cafeteria and in the finishing room. Tom worked on the paper machines while Karen worked in Tech control. When David was in Grade 12, he was a foreman in the finishing room. He supervised men who were nearly 50 years older than he was. I used to smile when David wanted to go to an adult movie. I would have to go to the theatre and sign him in. Then after the movie, he would go to work and supervise a crew of men.

When three children were going to University in Vancouver, Ted and I thought it would be wise to buy a house close to UBC and have all the children live at home during their university years. That summer everyone was at home, working shift work I stood by the stove all day, making meals and packing lunches at all hours. I would stay up, or at least be awakened as each one came home late, and then get up with the first one. If they did not get home when I expected them, I would worry. Finally, I realized how foolish this was. When they were in Vancouver, I did not worry about them. I believed they were responsible adults, but at home, I began to treat them as children again. Besides, it was exhausting! We decided that it was better to let the children have their independence.

Arlene became the only student on the academic programme in Grade Ten. We arranged for her to board with Ruth and Jim Robertson, our former next-door neighbours, and attend school in Coquitlam. Karen was in Grade Eleven and there were still several academic students in her class so we did not feel it was so imperative to move her.

Diane, Tom and David were all attending UBC and living together in an apartment on Cornwall Street, across the road from the ocean. The apartment was on the market for $23,000, but that price seemed much too expensive for an apartment. Little did we realize how much it would appreciate over the next 25 years.

Karen loved to sew, and in high school, made many of her own clothes. She always dressed in a feminine and fashionable style. Karen excelled in academic studies. Each assignment was completed as carefully as possible. Karen is a perfectionist.

Karen excelled in sports, particularly in running. Her extraordinarily long legs allowed her to race with speed and grace. Most of all, Karen loved to dance. Put a record on the turntable, and Karen would spin around in time to the beat, lost in her own world.

When Karen finished Grade 11, her marks were sufficiently high for her to move directly to Simon Fraser University without taking Grade Twelve. I guess it was just another example to prove to the Minister of Education that small schools can produce excellent students.

The first year Tom was at UBC, he met a special friend, Kico Gonzales. Tom encouraged him to come to work in the mill for the summer. Kico arrived with a long black serape and a huge Spanish style black hat which invited recognition by everyone who saw him. Kico was a writer and acquired enough insights of life in the mill and the eccentricities of many local people to flesh out several plots and characters in his writings.

Ted now had a new fish boat, "The Brownie Won" which he had commissioned in a shipyard in Vancouver. It had all the newest technology of the time, radar, and a sounder. These devices made it possible to image the bottom of the sea, to tell accurately the depth of the water, to tell if there were any rocks, and to see schools of fish. It also made it safer to travel in the fog, which is so common on the west coast.

One summer, Aunt Joyce, Mother's elder sister, came to visit. Ted and I took her out in our boat for a couple of days. She had, I think, a memorable holiday as we went to several isolated beaches, wandered about picking up driftwood and shells for the crafts she loved to do. We even brought home some pieces of trees over ten feet long, which sadly she could not take back to Penticton with her.

Brownie Won

On another occasion, we decided to go out for abalone. The best catches are made on a minus tide. Cove McDowell took his boat and the two families started out together. Mary Ann and Susan were on Uncle Cove's boat. When the wind began to rise, it got a little choppy so he tied both girls to the mast so he would not have to worry about them falling overboard. Karen and Arlene were on our boat. As we went through a narrow channel, and as the water was very low, Ted told the girls to lie on the bow and tell us when we came close to any rocks. They took their responsibility very seriously.

Shortly we felt a hard bump, and then one of them said, "We're close to the rock now."

And indeed, we were. We had to sit on the rock for several hours until the tide lifted and we could go safely through the passage.

Ted with a halibut

Another time the children wanted to go camping on King Island. They suggested Ted take them out in our boat, drop them off and return for them in a couple of days. We felt uneasy about this arrangement so decided we would take them out as they wished, drop them off, and Ted and I would anchor the boat at some distance from them. We put them off on their chosen camping spot, with their gear and lots of food. We also left them our skiff in case they needed to return to the boat for any reason.

We had hardly settled into our peaceful retreat, when we heard the sound of voices and noted the return of the skiff. The children wanted more food. They had lots of food, but wanted more good

197

stuff: chips and pop. After restocking their supply, they returned to their camp. We could see their fire in the distance and hear voices, though not their conversation and we went to bed. Not much later, the skiff returned with all the gear, the last of the food and several very wet people. It had begun to rain and no one was very interested in camping any more.

The bunk, which was comfortable for two people, now held four. Others were laying toes to nose on every available part of the cabin and deck. No one was comfortable. Then we realized we had a leak where some caulking must have come out of the hull. This was Saturday and the fishing opening for the week was 6 o'clock on Sunday night. There was no time to take the children back home.

We had to go directly to Namu, the closest place to get the boat repaired, and then begin the week's fishing with the whole family aboard the boat. It was not an easy job to set the gill net when there was no room to work. Certainly, Ted could not sleep between sets with so many people on board. It did not take long for a large family to eat Ted's week's supply of groceries. After one night's fishing, we returned to Ocean Falls.

The Mill, now owned by the NDP government, could not make a profit and once again the mill announced it would close the following March 31. This created a serious problem for the school. Finally, the decision was made to extend the school day so that the required number of hours of instruction could be completed by the end of March. Grade Twelve courses were semestered so students could write their government exams in January. Then they took their electives in February and March. No students failed any government exam. The concentrated schedule also seemed to ensure their success in the other areas.

On April 1, the boat to Vancouver pulled out of the dock, loaded with people leaving the town forever. A best selling book at this time was entitled "Ship of Fools" and a huge banner with this title was erected on the dock. As the ship left the harbour, passengers lined up on the dock and symbolically threw their umbrellas overboard. It was a fitting farewell to a town that had existed since the turn of the century.

198

It is significant to our family that Fred Brown, Ted's father, worked the first shift on the paper machine in 1916 and Tom worked the last shift on the same machine. Our family history was interwoven with the town's story.

Conditions in Ocean Falls continued to deteriorate. The superintendent, when he came to visit, commented that the town resembled a city ghetto. I agreed. It became increasingly apparent that I should find a position somewhere near the ocean so Ted could continue to fish from a home base.

Sooke School district had an advertisement in the Vancouver Sun for a Home Economics teacher. I wrote for an application. Within days, they phoned to say I was appointed to the district with a choice of either Dunsmuir or Belmont Seconday Schools. I selected Dunsmuir, as it was the smaller of the two. I was surprised not to have an interview before my appointment.

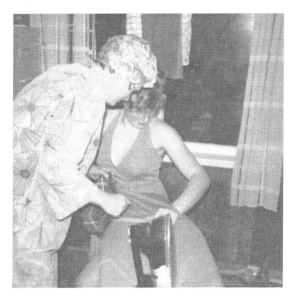

Joyce & Arlene
Almost ready for the dance -- Christmas 1973

Victoria
1974-1986

The first day of school at Dunsmuir Secondary, I set out in the early morning rush hour traffic. What a scary situation. I had never driven in heavy traffic before, never changed lanes, never stopped at a traffic light. By the time I got to school, my legs were shaking and I was completely unnerved. In fact, I was a menace on the road.

Worst of all, I realized I would have to return home the same way. "Would I have to wait for evening and the traffic thinned before I returned home?" I wondered. Each day I grew a little more confident.

A few weeks later Ted phoned from the wharf downtown to come and pick him up. Again, it was rush hour.

"I will come down about seven," I promised.

"And what do you think I will do for two hours?" he retorted grimly.

"But I don't do downtown yet," I replied somewhat hesitantly.

"That is the silliest thing I ever heard. I will expect you in about twenty minutes."

Obedient as always, I set out through the narrow streets, crowded with rush hour traffic, to the dock and rescued Ted from his enforced wait on the boat.

Gradually I was able to change lanes, take routes that included left as well as right turns, and even park in small spaces; but never to parallel park. That remained for the experts.

Susan, Ted, Karen
Mary Ann, Rhoda Brown, Joyce -- 1975

Our family at home was now diminished to three children as
Karen was attending Simon Fraser University in Burnaby. Arlene
and Susan were enrolled in Belmont High School which enrolled
about 1600 students. This number exceeded the entire population
of Ocean Falls. Several additions had been added to the school in
previous years so the total length was nearly a quarter of a mile.
Getting from class to class in the short period breaks was a
challenge. Soon both girls were involved in many activities and
did not seem to be worried by the large numbers of students.

Mary Ann went to Grade Six in Langford Elementary School. The first day of classes, she informed us she was the only person in her class who had both parents in their home.

"Don't be silly," I said, "You must have been mistaken."

She was correct. It was a low-income area with many broken families. Most homes had both a male and female present, but not necessarily the biological parents of the children.

Susan (13), Mary Ann (11), Arlene (16)

One day we stopped at a nearby garden to pick vegetables. The owner was amazed that Mary Ann had never seen vegetables growing in a garden. Her enthusiasm and wonder at seeing the crops inspired her to give Mary Ann a huge bag of vegetables. Mary Ann seemed to know, even then, how to get what she wanted.

Susan (16)

Susan is very creative. From an early age, she enjoyed constructing items from cloth, paint, beads and other craft supplies. She could make the simplest materials come alive in her hands; Susan could see the possibilities in these materials and interpret them. She was interested in pottery making and made many unique pieces.

In high school, Susan became interested in gymnastics. The living room became her work out area. Much effort went into developing a unique routine that was her individual creation.

Susan's gentle, loving nature was evident as a small child. These qualities drew friends to her and she, in turn, was a loyal friend to them. Her sense of fun and good humour along with her infectious laugh also attract people to her. I am glad her brothers and sisters plotted to bring her into our family.

Arlene
Valedictorian - Belmont High School
1976

Arlene was involved in many activities, most of which seemed to involve her in organizing events and keeping track of money. She was on the senior girl's basketball team. At graduation, Arlene was selected as valedictorian. She managed to maintain excellent grades while having a busy social life. These skills and talents lead to her acceptance to the University of BC under the Officer's Training Programme.

Ted and I had always dreamed of having a trip to Hawaii, but never thought it would happen. Although we had been away for a few days at a time, now and again, we had never had a major holiday.

Joyce & Ted – 25th Wedding Anniversary
Hawaii – 1976

For our twenty-fifth anniversary, our family gave us a two- week all expenses paid holiday to Hawaii. We spent one week in Honolulu and one week in Maui. Everything was a photo opportunity from the moment we received the typical lei greeting upon entering the airport, until we climbed aboard the homeward flight carrying a case of pineapples.

We decided to go on a moonlight cruise to celebrate New Year's Eve. Dine and dance aboard a catamaran, see the beautiful sunset, have a night to remember, said the brochures.

Our first intimation that not all might be as expected happened as we drove up to the dock and saw a Chubby Chicken truck dropping off trays of food.

We piled on board, not to sit on the deck, but crouched below decks, in what surely must have resembled steerage conditions in the old slave ships. There was no room to move, as we pressed even closer together to let late- comers join us. There might have been dancing, as a guitar player was on board, but the space for dancing was covered with passengers squatting on the deck -no chairs for them, of course, because their space was the designated dance floor.

From the lower deck we could not see the scenery as the port holes were above eye level. The sea was perfectly flat until one small swell approached us. For those of us used to being on the water, we hardly felt the boat rise and fall.

Immediately several women screamed in panic and a small child sitting next to me became sea sick, vomiting down my evening dress. The child's Mother tried to wipe me with a Kleenex, but paper is not a deodorizer.

As we floated along, increasingly hot and uncomfortable, the crew decided to serve us our romantic dinner for two. I guess that meant they carried two plates at a time. The small girl could not eat so her mother placed her plate on a narrow shelf just above her head. When I turned to look, I saw several cockroaches crawling on the dish. My meal suddenly became less appetizing. Still we ploughed mercilessly onwards. At about 8 o'clock, the boat changed direction and began to return to port.

We had expected to see the New Year in aboard the boat, but luckily, it was returning after only two hours. It had other tourists to pick up for the next moonlight cruise. New Year's Eve came only once a year for those greedy entrepreneurs.

We had a wonderful holiday and enjoyed all the typical tourist sights, but we agreed that we would never again spend Christmas away from our children.

Our life fell into a pattern. Ted fished and did electrical contracting in the winter. I went to school and then to Summer School, the children continued their own lives separate from ours. They can write their own stories of school, careers, marriages and babies. These years in Victoria are a blur as one event followed another in rapid succession.

1978 marked a turning point in my life. That year I completed my BED in Secondary Education. For fourteen years, I had taken correspondence courses, and gone to summer School when I could, to complete my degree. At first, it seemed like an impossible goal, but as I eventually finished one year at a time, the dream was accomplished.

Diane completed her Home Economics degree before I did and was teaching in Prince George. We began the collaboration we continued for several years. As we taught the same courses, Family Studies, and Textiles, we planned our units together, each helping the other with new ideas and resources to make our lessons more interesting.

We were having some personal problems and I prayed for a solution. Soon the missionaries from the Church of Jesus Christ of Latter-day Saints knocked at our door. I realized as soon as I opened the door that my answer lay in joining the church. There must have been a residual thought from their visits to us in Penticton more than twenty years previously. I did not accept this idea, nor tell the Elders my impression, but did invite them in and soon received the lessons.

Joyce - Staff picture Dunsmuir Secondary School --1980

I did not accept baptism. Why would I join another church? I regularly attended the United Church. I had friends there. I was not sure I wanted to stop drinking tea and coffee. How could I afford to tithe? Still the missionaries continued to visit and I continued to ask obtuse questions.

Eventually, a voice spoke to me so clearly, "Joyce, Why are you being so silly? You know the gospel is true. Why won't you be baptized?"

I followed these promptings of the Spirit and I was baptized a few days later, 28 September 1978. It was the wisest thing I have ever done. I knew the Gospel was true and I could not deny it.

Ted also began to take the discussions and set a date for baptism the following April. Fate intervened. He was feeling somewhat tired for no apparent reason and went to the doctor for an examination.

"You are not going home," said the doctor, "but must stay in the hospital until you have open heart surgery."

Ted had no idea until then that he had any heart problem. Three days later, he had a triple by-pass. The technique was relatively new then and the risk was very high that he would not survive.

The first day following surgery, only I was allowed to visit and only for two minutes at a time. I will never forget the sight of him immediately after the operation, with wires and tubes from every possible location.

Doctors removed a vein from his ankle almost to the groin, and used it to replace the arteries in his heart.

"This replacement will last about five years," the doctor told me. "Then he will require another similar operation."

Ted recovered slowly but steadily. He was unable to work for almost a year and then was never able to do the heavy work of a fisherman or electrician again. It was a very sad day when he sold his boat.

One side effect of the surgery was that Ted's hair, which had become quite grey, came in jet black. Later, as he aged, people would tell him he should stop dying his hair, as it did not look natural.

Another side effect was the loss of memory. Several months after the surgery, he said to me that it was strange that none of the children had come to visit him when he had his surgery. This was not true; they had all come home to see him except Susan who was a Rotary Exchange student in Liege, Belgium. Ted's memory never returned completely after this operation.

As soon as Ted had healed sufficiently, he was baptized in June 1979.

While Ted was still in the hospital, my parents celebrated their fiftieth wedding anniversary. It was a major event with all the family there except Ted and Susan.

Duncan McDonald, Mother, Dad
50th Wedding Anniversary

Joyce telling stories

*Five Generations: Joyce, David, Rose & Joel Garr
Grandma Pridmore, Mother -- 1979*

*Five Generations: Mother, Grandma Pridmore,
Crystal & Karen Stranaghan, Joyce- 1979*

Soon I became engulfed in the life of the church. I was a member for only a short time before I was called to teach a Young Women's class. This followed soon after by the calling to be Young Women's President. I did not realize that I was expected to go to Girls' Camp that summer. I suggested to Bishop Nelson that I thought Girls' Camp would be better undertaken by a young woman, and not a grandmother, (Joel, David's son, our first grandchild, was a new baby) but he was unmoved.

Actually, I went to girl's camp twice, the only camping experiences of my life, and had great fun. I even worked alongside the girls and got my first year and second- year badges.

I had been to Relief Society meetings only a few times prior to my calling in the Young Women's programme. You can appreciate how surprised I was to be called as the Relief Society President. I knew nothing, except in the broadest terms, of what they did. I did not even know how they conducted their Sunday meetings. With the help of two counsellors, Carol Stiles and Donna Buettner, I managed to learn.

On December 26, 1980, my mother had an aneurysm and died suddenly. It was a terrible shock. She had not been feeling too well before Christmas, so for the first time in her life, had spent a few days in the hospital. The doctor thought she had the flu and was well enough to come home. Dad was planning to go to Greenwood for his brother, Joe McDonald's, funeral and I was on my way to stay with Mother until Dad returned. We were in Nanaimo, waiting for the ferry when we were paged to report for a phone message. We were told that Mother had died unexpectedly. I never go to the ferry without remembering that day.

Aunt Joyce and I, the two Joyce Browns, representing the oldest of our generations, spoke at Mother's funeral. I did not think I would be able to do that, but I know we are always given strength to do what must be done.

I know we will live together someday and that gives me great comfort and strength when I think of those of our families who have passed away.

Mother's Family – The Pridmores: Ernie & Ruth McKillop,
Grandma, Aunt Joyce Brown, Dad & Mother -- Spring 1979

The year 1981 marked Grandma Pridmore's 100th birthday. For many years after Grandpa died, she spent her life travelling from one daughter to the next. In the winter, she stayed with her daughter, Joyce Brown, in Penticton. In the spring, she visited my mother in Abbotsford. Later when the weather improved on the prairies, she spent the summer with her daughter, Ruth McKillop in Regina or at the lake near Arcola. Grandma celebrated her 100th birthday at each of her "homes" with the family and friends she knew there. What a full life she had lived. She had ridden in a horse-drawn coach in Victorian England; she had travelled by steam train across Canada to Saskatchewan soon after it became a province; she had flown in a jet plane.

Grandma remained interested in everything around her. She read, kept informed of political events and continued to knit and crochet at this advanced age. Grandma lived to be 102 years old.

Until she died, she lived with her family, surrounded by those she loved and those who loved and cared for her.

Grandma Pridmore's 100th Birthday—1981

Ted & Joyce – 30th Wedding Anniversary -- 1981

United Church, Arcola, Saskatchewan
Dedicated to the memory of
Thomas & Emma Pridmore & Bessie Mae McDonald
Commissioned in England by Aunt Joyce

Fort McMurray
1986-1995

David was negotiating to purchase an AMJ Campbell franchise in Fort McMurray. This moving company was affiliated with Atlas Moving Company, a major leader in its field. He suggested Ted and I might want to join him as part of his staff.

We would never have considered moving north if we had not spent the previous Christmas in North Bay with Arlene and Bill. The temperatures lowered to -25 degrees while we were there and we survived. We even went cross-country skiing without freezing to death. Our holiday proved to us that we had the right stuff to live in the north. We agreed to go. It would be an adventure.

We sold our two houses, one a rental and another we lived in; I retired from teaching and off we went As Ted had left a few months before I finished school, Mary Ann drove with me to Fort McMurray. It seemed a much longer distance than I expected.

When we got as far as Wandering River, there were no longer many houses or farms. After about 100 kilometres, we reached another small community, Marianna Lake, with a gas station and a coffee shop. A sign warned us there would not be another stop for a further 100 kilometres. For miles, there was nothing to see but stunted trees, muskeg and the occasional vehicle, usually a truck, meeting us en route.

Eventually we came to the outskirts of Fort McMurray, with the usual warehouse sprawl in sight. The city itself rests in a basin at the foot of a steep hill. Three rivers meet at Fort McMurray, the Athabaska, the Clearwater and the Horse.

Fort McMurray's location made it the centre of fur trading in the early days. Even today, the Athabaska River is a busy trade route in the summer taking fuel and other goods down the river to Fort Chippewa and other northern communities. In the winter, the barges and freight carriers sit on land in Fort McMurray awaiting the spring break-up.

After almost two hundred kilometres of wilderness, suddenly we could see a well-planned city of about 35,000 people. Several major subdivisions are almost hidden from first sight in Beaconhill, Thickwood and Abasand. The original town of Waterways is only a short distance from the newer city of Fort McMurray.

Dragline at Syncrude
Boom is the length of a football field

The city, in 1986, was supported by two major tar sands developments, Syncrude and Suncor. In the summer months, a tour bus took visitors to the mining sites. It was the largest development of its kind in the world. Four gigantic cranes, each with a boom as long as a football field scooped up the tar sand in buckets that held the volume of a house and placed it either in enormous trucks or on conveyor belts. From a distance, you could see the bulldozers working around the cranes to keep the ground flat in the working area: they seemed like dinky toys. Up close, they were the largest bulldozers on the market. The cranes operated by electricity, generated on site. Each crane was plugged in, like some enormous toaster.

Near the plant were huge white sand dunes, waste left after the heavy oil was removed. As the mining played out in one area, the pit was filled in and the land returned to its natural state. A nursery supplied seedling trees to reforest the mined area. Bison, cared for by the local natives, were introduced to roam on the site.

Ted & Gregory Brown
Oil Sands Interpretive Centre, Fort McMurray -- 1994

The first summer of operation, the moving business was a family affair. Margaret, Tom's wife, worked in the office while Tom and David were drivers. Mark Rutledge, Diane's husband, was hired as a salesman. Ted worked on the trucks and helped in the warehouse. Margaret trained me in the office routines and taught me how to do the paperwork. The operation was more complicated than I had thought it would be as there was a complex method of splitting the distribution of revenue depending on how the shipment was handled, who booked it, who packed it and how many different drivers handled and unpacked the freight.

The first year was reasonably profitable, but the next year was more difficult. A strike at Suncor and a slowdown in the general economy put a heavy strain on the business. We were getting quite a bit of business through Lloydminster and we thought if we had a warehouse and office there, we could work the two offices together profitably. Ted and I went to Lloydminster and set up an office while I continued to do the books for both operations. Lloydminster office was going smoothly. We could find good crews to pack and swamp but the business was not going smoothly in Fort McMurray. Because the population base was larger there, we decided to sell the Lloydminster franchise and return to Fort McMurray and salvage what we could of that business.

In a convoluted moving deal, we took in trade a run down three-bedroom mobile home in the downtown area. It was almost beyond redemption, but Ted began to repair and paint and slowly it became liveable. It had a basement suite, which we rented. Our first renters were young men who were not satisfactory tenants for a variety of reasons, but mostly because they did not pay their rent. Eventually we rented to an older woman, Marion Christopherson, who became a dear friend.

In September 1989, I had a call from a friend, Adina Hudkins, the secretary at Westwood High School. She knew I was a retired Home Economics teacher and wondered if I would consider substituting for two weeks as the Home Economics teacher, Dianne Clark-Jones, was ill and unable to begin the school year. As the moving business slowed off in the fall, I thought I could do this and my office work. I met the principal, Les Hansen, and agreed to this short contract. Dianne was not well enough to teach until just before Christmas.

Ted fixing up the house

In January I got another call from Les Hansen asking me to teach part time starting February first. As this was for just one block a day, he also arranged with the Catholic Board for me to teach one block a day at Father Mercredi High School. This I did, teaching at two schools each morning, and then returning to the office each afternoon.

The next September I returned to Westwood High School as the librarian. Later I also taught some Foods Studies. My two-week substitution contract turned into six years completed before I retired again in 1995.

There were two public high Schools in Fort McMurray. Diane taught Food Studies at Composite High School and I taught the same courses at Westwood High School. As we had previously done when Diane taught in Prince George and I taught in Sooke, we planned our lessons cooperatively, so students at both schools had identical lessons. It facilitated transfers of students from one school to the other. Later, we developed individualized modules so students could work independently and at their own rate in classes that often included students at different grade levels. From this beginning, Diane expanded and refined the modules that she marketed under the dR Publishing label.

Joyce & Ted
Caribbean Cruise – 1987

During these years, Ted and I had several more extensive holidays. In 1987, we went for a Caribbean cruise on the Dutch vessel, Voordam. We flew to Fort Lauderdale, and then sailed to the Virgin Islands and Puerto Rico. We enjoyed the nightclub acts aboard ship and marvelled at the luxurious meals. On shore, we toured an aquarium, saw the fortifications in San Juan and relaxed in the summer-like heat compared to the prairies winter cold.

In 1991, Ted and I went to Germany to visit Arlene and her family. We travelled to Berlin by train with Arlene and Natasha, just a few weeks old. We could see the contrast between East and West Germany. Suddenly as we crossed the border, the lush farms and well cared for homes of the west turned into derelict buildings and spotty fields of corn. Despite that, the farmhouses all had cheerful beds of flowers around them. The contrast between East and West Berlin was obvious everywhere we went. The run down streets; the empty shops, the apartment buildings in obvious disrepair all attested to the poverty of East Berlin.

The Berlin Wall was torn down just a short time before we arrived. Everywhere we went, there were peddlers at the sides of the roads with tables selling pieces of the wall covered with coloured snatches of graffiti. In other places, there were sellers with little scraps of what they claimed were parts of the wall, spread out on blankets. However, there were no markings on the bits of concrete and we wondered if they were just random pieces of broken concrete selected to entice unsuspecting tourists to part with their money.

We saw gypsy caravans as well. At one place, we saw a family come out of a van. The mother led a small child to a bridge, muddied up her face and mussed her hair. Then she placed a sign beside the child requesting donations. The other children, also in begging attire, were placed here and there nearby. We did see the Olympic Stadium, the Brandenburg Monument, and the famous Linden trees that lined the city streets.

Ted and I also went by train along the banks of the Rhine River to the temple in Freiberg, Germany. In the distance, we could see many castles that looked as if they were part of a Walt Disney movie.

The temple had a dormitory with three bunk beds in each room. Patrons cooked their own meals in a communal kitchen. We did not know we were supposed to bring our own food and soap. Kind people shared with us. We had one session in German with earphones, but I decided to have the next session in Spanish. It was enough like French that I could follow the presentation and was easier than trying to cope with the wires from the phone.

The next year I went again to Germany, but this time by myself. Arlene and I left her family at home and she and I went to England. At Lincoln, we visited the Cathedral where a symphony concert was in progress. We went down in the basement area and looked at the crypts of famous people. A man in his church raiment requested we leave, as the cathedral was not open to the public. As he approached us, he identified himself as "Tom, the Verger."

After we left Arlene said, "I wonder why he told us he was a virgin?" Now it was my turn to explain the difference between a verger and a virgin.

We also went to Collingham, where my Grandmother Pridmore was born. Here we did find mother's cousin, Sue Pridmore, and her family. They made us very welcome. We slept in the bed in which our great-grandparents had slept. The stairs were too narrow to move a bed, so the boards were brought through the window and the bed was constructed in the place where it remains to this day.

Our newfound relatives took us to Nottingham Castle. It was on these grounds that Grandma Pridmore used to push mother in her pram.

We also went to Sherwood Forest to see the home of Robin Hood and his Merry Men. Of course, the tree famed in the legend is not still standing, but there are many huge oak trees, which are like that famed tree, must have been. Trees are fenced off as countless footsteps compacted the ground too much, threatening the lives of the trees.

Naturally, there is a gift shop connected with the site. I bought a felt cap, and a quiver with a bow and arrow to take home to Derek, Tom's son, as it was soon his birthday. When we got to Heathrow airport, I was told I could not take the bow and arrow on the plane as it was a dangerous weapon.

Sherwood Forest

As we stood at the counter protesting this ruling, a supervisor came to the area. We explained our problem once more.

Looking as stern as he could, he turned to Arlene. "And who do you think you are," he asked, "Maid Marion?"

Eventually, the supervisor allowed us to take our dangerous weapon on board, but we had to sit in a special waiting room away from all other passengers until flight time. I wonder what would happen now as the danger of terrorist attack has intensified.

Derek Brown with his Robin Hood outfit
1991

August 7, 1993 was an unhappy day. My father had suffered from Alzheimer's disease for several years. For several years after mother's death, he lived with my brother, Michael, and his wife, Ann, but eventually moved to a senior's facility in Abbotsford where he could have the care he required as he became less able to look after himself. It was sad to see a proud and independent man become a shell of his former self. He lived to be eighty-six years of age, the last thirteen years without Mother. I am sure they were lonely years for him.

Joyce & Dad Taken shortly before Dad's death

Joyce, Ian, Don, Michael, Ruth --August 10, 1993

Dad's memorial service - held on the lawn at Michael & Ann's
Back: Karen & Glen Stranaghan, Tom, David, Joel Garr
Middle: Mary Ann Tennent, Crystal Stranaghan,
Margaret Brown, Diane Rutledge, Joyce, Ted
Front: Arlana Tennent, Aaron Stranaghan,
Derek, Alex & Greg Brown
August 10, 1993

From the time we joined the church, we had planned to serve a mission. As my sixty-fifth birthday approached, it seemed the right time to make this dream a reality. When I retired for the second time, I was surprised to realize I had taught in each of the past six decades -1949 -1995.

As Ted and I had our birthday on the same day, May 8, Diane ordered a special cake decorated with "Happy 135th Birthday." When I went into the Safeway store to pick it up, all the bakery staff were lined up waiting to see me. They had never seen anyone 135 years old before. It was really an event to reach such an age, even though it took the total of both our ages to achieve it.

We sold our house, in Fort McMurray, rented out a house we owned in Saskatoon, put our furniture in storage, and made plans to leave for the Mission Training Centre in Provo, Utah.

Ted & Joyce: Happy 135th Birthday
May 8, 1995

Joyce
Westwood High School library

*Joyce, Ruth
McKillop, Joyce
Brown
August 1991*

*Ted & Joyce
40th Wedding
Anniversary --
1991*

Mississauga
1995-1997

Before leaving for the Missionary Training Centre in Provo, Utah, we planned to make a visit to each of our children The night we got to Victoria was stormy with fierce winds and heavy rain. As we drove under an overpass and turned up hill to enter the city, a car driven by a teenaged girl, crossed the dividing line and smashed into the front of our car, causing several thousand dollars damage. Although I did not realize it, the force of the impact caused the seat belt to crush my chest resulting in three cracked ribs.

The repair shop informed us that by the time they ordered parts and did the necessary repairs, we would be without a car for at least six weeks.

"I do not think you understand," Ted said. "We are leaving for Utah in three weeks in this car. It has to be repaired by then. We are flying to Ottawa tomorrow and when we get back, I expect the car to be ready."

"We will do our best," the mechanic replied. "But we have never been able to get parts and do this big a job in such a short time."

"We will be back in two weeks to pick up our car." Ted responded emphatically, as we left.

And in the first of many miracles we encountered on our Mission, the car was ready in time to leave at the beginning of October.

I was in quite a bit of pain from my ribs, but that hardly detracted from our trip. Fall was just beginning and the hills were covered with the changing colours. We stopped at Idaho Falls to seek directions. Imagine our surprise to discover that the driver was Thelma Bigalow, whom we had known when she and her husband were lighthouse keepers near Shearwater. Their children later came to school in Ocean Falls, and were friends of our children

In Provo, the senior missionaries lived in a motel, which had been remodelled to serve as the senior's training centre. It had many classrooms in which we were taught what was required to serve as proselyting missionaries. We worked in small groups with returned missionaries practicing the missionary discussions.

A highlight was meeting and being instructed by church leaders. At one meeting, we joined with the younger missionaries. What a thrill to hear over two thousand missionaries sing the hymn, "Called to Serve". Later, we discovered this hymn was the official Toronto East Mission song, with added verses making it specific to the mission area.

Joyce & Ted -- Provo, Utah, 1995

After about a week, we set off for Toronto. From Salt Lake, we travelled almost directly east through Wyoming, Nebraska, Iowa, Illinois, then across the tip of Indiana to the border at Detroit and back to Canada once more.

We came to understand why Americans celebrate Thanksgiving in November, not October, as we do in Canada. While harvesting was complete on the Canadian prairies when we left home, it was just beginning on the American plains.

We stayed overnight in a hotel in Toronto and set out early for our meeting in the Mission home. After over two hours in rush hour traffic we arrived, somewhat frazzled and certainly stressed after the drive through heavy traffic, Trucks and cars weaving in and out on the 401 at maximum speeds, lanes ending unexpectedly, insecurity as to where to turn all added to our stress. It took us some time to adjust to the traffic.

Mission President and Sister Boyer welcomed all the newly arrived missionaries. We had an orientation meeting, lunch, and received our ward assignment. Ted and I were sent to the Mississauga Ward. New friends, from the MTC, Girt and Ine Christensen from Maple Ridge, BC, were assigned to the neighbouring Weston Ward.

Mississauga is a bedroom community for Toronto. As a planned community, there are huge subdivisions of brick houses surrounded with well-maintained gardens. Wide streets many of which are lined with maple trees, generous manicured boulevards, and many public parks make Mississauga a very attractive area.

Housing was expensive and suites appropriate for missionaries were difficult to find. A real estate agent, a member of the church, found us a basement suite for $525 per month. It consisted of one large room with a bathroom and closet off to one side. There was also a small kitchenette area with a sink, a shelf above it for groceries, and an apartment-size fridge and stove. There was no furniture. We bought foam for a bed, a chrome table with two chairs and a small dresser from a second hand store. Later, members gave us a bed, a Lazy Boy chair and a small cupboard in which we kept papers and such small items.

We decided, before we left home, that we would live just as the younger missionaries. We would keep the same hours, would not have a television, nor would we read beyond the prescribed books.

We got up at 6 o'clock, had breakfast, then read the Book of Mormon for one half hour, practiced our discussions and planned for our day. By 9 o'clock, we left our room and set out on our appointments. If we did not have zone meetings or similar events, we tried to set up at least six appointments each day: two each in the morning, afternoon and evening. In the summer, when the days were pleasant, we packed a lunch and ate in a park or by the shore of Lake Ontario. We were home each night by nine with lights out by 10 o'clock.

Monday was preparation day. At this time, we bought our groceries, did laundry, wrote letters and visited various tourist attractions around Toronto. In the evening, we were expected to be back at work.

Each Wednesday we worked in the Bishop's Storehouse in Etobicoke, another suburb of Toronto. This warehouse served as the distribution centre for a wide area both east and west of Toronto, for those needing welfare help. We were impressed with the variety and quality of the products, many grown on church-owned farms and canned in church operated factories. Members volunteered their labour for church welfare at these facilities. In St. Catharines, there was a large orchard where volunteers from the Mississauga Stake worked pruning, weeding and picking apples and pears.

In other food banks, patrons are given whatever food is donated. Depending on these donations, the foods distributed may not necessarily be nutritious nor of a high quality. This was not the case in the Bishop's Storehouse.

Ward Bishops decided which families were in need of help. Then the Relief Society President visited the member's home and assessed the family's need. Nutritious meals were planned, with consideration for the family's preferences, and then the necessary foods were ordered. Cleaning supplies and personal products were also included in the order.

From the warehouse, the orders were filled and delivered by truck to the various meeting houses, where the members could pick up their orders. Groceries from the storehouse are given freely to those in need, but those who can , are expected to help repay by working in the storehouse, by filling orders, refilling shelves or by doing appropriate service in their own wards. All recipients are expected to work if they are physically able to do so.

At lunchtime a meal made completely of the foods available in the Storehouse, was served to the workers. This had many purposes: it taught how to prepare simple nutritious meals from basic ingredients, how to set the table, and how to serve the meal attractively. The noontime meal was also a source of friendship and fellowship to members who may not have known many people in their community.

Another rule was that the missionaries were never away from their companion. At first, this was difficult as we were used to each doing our own thing for the day, then spending the evening together.

Soon after we arrived, we needed to get our hair cut. We looked for a salon that accepted both men and women. We soon found such a shop, operated by a Chinese couple whose knowledge of English was very limited. I had previously had my hair styled in Victoria in what I thought was quite a fashionable style. I explained carefully that I wanted my hair cut exactly as it was then done. The stylist looked at me and seemed to comprehend what I meant.

"Exactly the same," she repeated running her fingers through my hair while nodding her head knowingly.

In a while, she passed me the mirror to admire the new haircut. I looked at the front, and then slowly turned to look at the back. Yes, she was right it was exactly the same…as Ted's. Oh, well, in just a few weeks it grew back again.

When we first arrived, the ward list had been lost because of a computer glitch. We were given an old list with about thirty names on it. It was suggested we could start with this and we would get a complete ward list in a few days. No one told us what to do. It was assumed as Senior Missionaries we could assess what might be needed and do it.

We set out with our list, and approached the first house, a palatial brick home in an upscale neighbourhood. When the door opened, there stood a woman with two Rottweiler dogs on chains, growling and straining to be let free. Bravely, we stated who we were. Angrily, the woman accused the church of harassing her. She had never belonged to the church, she never would, and if we did not leave immediately, she would not only call the police, but would release her dogs. I guessed this action would prove her point. It did not take us long to get the idea, and we left immediately. Somewhat shaken by this experience we wondered if we had made a wise decision to accept a mission call. Was this what our life would be like for another eighteen months? We had never thought our lives would be threatened.

The following afternoon, at the next name on our list, we discovered no one at home, but a note on the door stated that someone would be back soon. The note was certainly not for us; no one knew we were coming. About two blocks away we saw a woman hurrying along the side of the street.

"Stop," I said to Ted. "That is the lady whom we were supposed to meet."

He gave me a strange look, but obeyed my instructions. Sure enough, it was Melva Durie, who became one of our closest friends. It was a great lesson to us of how our Heavenly Father guided and directed us to those who needed to hear of the Gospel. We had many such experiences as our mission continued. We learned to follow the promptings of the Spirit; we never again had any frightening ferocious dog experiences.

Our days and weeks began to fall into a pattern. We taught the New Member discussions, visited the sick in the hospital, searched out recent move-ins and visited the less active. We especially enjoyed teaching the Temple preparation classes. We were privileged to take many to the Temple for the first time. The Toronto Temple was only twenty minutes from Mississauga, so we often took investigators to the temple to visit the grounds and to go into the sitting area within the temple.

Monica Fagan & Joyce
Toronto Temple

A highlight of our Mission was a trip to Palmyra to attend the pageant. We, with Elder and Sister Christensen, chartered a bus and invited recent converts and investigators to go to Palmyra for the day. We visited the Sacred Grove where Joseph Smith in answer to prayer, saw God, the Father, and Jesus Christ. From this beginning, the Church of Jesus Christ of Latter-day Saints was established. We also saw the house in which Joseph Smith and his family lived, the print shop where the Book of Mormon was first published and toured the Visitor's Centre.

The most moving event was the pageant which told the story of the Book of Mormon. All day the weather had been cold, windy and rainy. We had a tarp wrapped around us to keep out the wet. We huddled together thinking how uncomfortable we were. About twenty minutes before the pageant was to begin, it stopped

237

raining, the wind became calm, and the sun came out. More than 7000 people were sitting on chairs on the flat plain in front of the Hill Cumorah. We could see the statue of the Angel Moroni gleaming gold as the evening sun shone on it. Eventually, the sun began to set until only Moroni could be seen. As the last glimmer of gold disappeared, we could see trumpeters on the hill summoning the tribes of Israel to gather. Over 600 actors in lavish costumes marched in under the flags of the 12 tribes of Israel, down the aisles of the audience and onto the stage. The finale where Christ appears in the Americas is particularly dramatic. Few people were unmoved.

During many of the hours before the presentation, the actors mingled among the audience. They remained in character as they answered questions and posed for photo opportunities with the patrons. Innumerable missionaries also were available to answer questions.

Many families went to Palmyra for their summer vacations to participate in the production. Actors, costume makers, set designers and work crews of all kinds were needed. Many special effects technicians from Hollywood are members who donated their expertise for the pageant.

While we were in Toronto, David had open-heart surgery in Saskatoon. Following his surgery, he came to Toronto to visit us for a few days. We had special permission to drive him to Ottawa where we visited with Arlene and her family. On another occasion Arlene, Bill and their three children stayed overnight in our little room. We were very crowded, but no more than if we had been in a tent. Toronto is truly a crossroad, as we also saw Tom and Margaret as they stopped over on a trip to the Caribbean.

The only cloud on our mission was Ted's health. About five months before we were to come home, Ted went to a heart specialist, who advised Ted that the artery in his heart, which had been replaced in 1979, had deteriorated and advised him to have open-heart surgery immediately. Ted told him that if he required surgery he would prefer to have it done at home. The doctor told him he should return immediately home with a nurse to accompany him, and arrange for surgery. The doctor said the artery could come "apart" at any time.

Ted said he would not return home without completing our mission, and we would just let things happen as they would. He said he would never go through what he had with the first heart operation. At that time, he had not been able to work for a year. He was afraid that the lack of oxygen that might happen during the surgery would cause even more loss of memory than had occurred during his first surgery. He was not prepared to accept that risk. He would not undergo surgery.

We continued to work as hard as we had done before the visit to the doctor, but each day we wondered if that day would be Ted's last one on this earth.

We tried to visit all the ward members before we came home. We had been shown so much kindness and love. Toronto is the most cosmopolitan city in the world. We had eaten traditional dishes from countries as diverse as Zaire, Jamaica, Russia, Guyana, Iran, Pakistan, Chile, and India. We came to understand what is meant by the expression "Joy in the Lord."

On the first week in March, we left for home. We went to Ottawa to say good-bye to Arlene's family. Would Ted ever see them again? Then we headed south to the United States where the roads were better than those in northern Ontario where it was still winter.

It was our intention to travel west as far as Fargo, North Dakota, crossing the Red River near there, then travel north-west to Minot, North Dakota and straight north to Saskatchewan and Fort McMurray. However, our plans were to change dramatically. The Red River was flooding and we could not cross at Fargo. We continued north, trying to cross the Red River at several places, but the waters were rising too fast. We dared not stop. The water was lapping at the edge of the road and all the surrounding fields were submerged. Eventually we reached Canada, just south of Winnipeg. The waters pursued us as we continued to go west until we were exhausted. Finally, we stopped for the night, or what was left of it.

In the morning, we set out again on this narrow secondary road. From the corner of my eye, I caught a road sign "Grande Clariére", the name of the town where Ted's mother was born. We had never been able to find it. She said it was near Winnipeg and we had reluctantly concluded it must have been absorbed into Winnipeg many years ago. We travelled along a country road to Grande Clariére, several miles off the secondary road we had first followed. Although it had once been a town with several stores and a garage, it now had only a church and two or three houses. A local man, standing by his car as we approached, was an old timer who pointed out where the Hatch family once lived. A family mystery was solved, thanks to a flood, which drove us hundreds of miles from our original destination.

Joyce at Grandma & Grandpa Pridmore's former home
Arcola -- 1997

Saskatoon
1997 - 2002

After returning to Fort McMurray to visit our family and friends, we gave our homecoming talks at church and reported on our many experiences in the mission field. Mere words could not express the joy we felt serving, nor the love and kindness that was given to us in Mississauga.

We decided to move into the house on Cumberland Avenue in Saskatoon that had been rented while we were on our mission. At first, we moved into the basement suite with our grandson, Joel. Many minor repairs were needed. Ted did these, and then repainted the entire suite. Then it was time to evict our tenants and move upstairs.

2518 Cumberland Avenue

For two years, we had lived with just the items we could put into our car. Now we moved several thousands of pounds of household goods out of storage and into our house. We wondered if we really needed so much "stuff". We had managed quite well with practically no material goods. It is amazing how much less work there is to do when your possessions are minimized.

All winter Ted worked on the house and when spring arrived, he spent all his time landscaping and developing a large vegetable garden. His happiest times were spent working there.

Ted in the garden

We knew that each day could be the last day. We made every effort to have all our business affairs in order. Ted attempted to

242

have the house and yard in perfect shape so I could manage easily when I must do this work alone.

Despite this cloud hanging over us, we became even closer as we talked about our life together, the problems we had endured and overcome and, especially, we talked about our children and grandchildren who had given us so much joy and pride.

In the summer of 1998, we went to a Brown family reunion at the home of Ted's sister, Grace and her husband, George Hennessey, in Falkland, BC. Our grandson, Joel Garr, was our designated driver. We also took James Rutledge, another grandson, and Ted's cousin Idamay Leech, from Kelvington, SK. It was the first time she had seen her cousins, Grace and George Brown, since they were small children. We watched the Falkland 100th Birthday Parade which Joel and James joined, racing along on their rollerblades. Mostly we just ate and visited and ate some more. There was never a shortage of food at a Brown gathering.

Ted & Joel Garr

September 21st began like any other beautiful autumn day. Ted kissed me good-bye, as he always did before going out to work. The garden was almost finished, but there were a few carrots left to pull. At about 10, I went out to have a little visit, but could not see him at first. The carrots were washed, sitting on the patio, but no sign of Ted. Then, I saw the gate to the back alley was ajar.

243

Lying in the open gateway was a vial of nitro glycerine which Ted always carried with him. Looking further, I saw him lying in the lane. By the contortion of his body, I knew that the unthinkable had happened and that he was gone. Nevertheless, I phoned 911 and the ambulance came within minutes. Although the paramedics tried to start his heart, I knew it was futile

When Ted first had open-heart surgery in 1979, the doctor told him he would possibly live five years. Almost 20 years later, another doctor told him he would not live long enough to complete his mission. He had lived a year and half longer than this final warning. Ted had been given a gift of 20 years that he did not expect. We knew, for years, that each day could be the last and we tried to make these last years have value and meaning.

For the first time in many years, our family was together. After a family service at the cemetery, we returned to the chapel for the public service. Although I felt distraught at the gravesite, I felt a great feeling of peace as the familiar prelude music was played. Two of Ted's favourite hymns were sung – "I Stand All Amazed" and "Amazing Grace". Tom and David spoke about their father. James Rutledge, a grandson, talked about his grandfather as a role model. Arlene read a tribute written by Karen Rutledge. As part of the programme, Jessica Jaques, a granddaughter, sang the theme song from the movie, Titanic, "My Heart Will Go On" accompanied by Karen Rutledge on her flute.

On the gravestone, I placed a bronze plaque with the scene of a small boat approaching a lighthouse, symbolic of the years Ted spent by the ocean, as well as the light of the Saviour, which guides us to eternal life. Engraved is the motto "Families Are Forever". I know this is true. Someday we will all be together with those whom we have loved in this life. This knowledge sustains me.

I was given a bouquet from my bother, Ian, and his wife, Carmel. In it were several large sunflowers. I decided to take them to put on Ted's grave. As I placed the flowers in the vase, two butterflies settled on the blossoms. I wandered away for a few minutes, lost in contemplation. When I returned, only one butterfly remained on the flower. Somehow, it seemed symbolic of the new life, which I must make for myself. Alone.

So Far

I have lived in 29 homes and 4 provinces.

I have taught all grades, from 1 to 12, in 8 schools during 6 decades.

During 47 years of marriage, Ted and I raised 7 children.

So far, I have 25 grandchildren and 8 great grandchildren and look forward to many more.

So far, I am well on my way to fulfilling my goal of having 100 descendents. I know my family will help me realize this dream as they have so many other dreams.

Mary Ann, David, Tom, Arlene, Karen, Diane, Joyce, Susan
Karen & Glen's 25th Wedding Anniversary -- August 2000

A Letter to My Family

Dreams can come true
It can happen to you
If you're young at heart

Many years ago, I made a suggestion to your Dad that when we retired we should get a motorcycle with a sidecar and travel across Canada.

"That way we could really see the countryside," I stated.

"Oh, you'd see the country all right," Dad retorted. "Every bug and fly from here to Halifax would be stuck in your teeth."

"But I would have goggles," I answered emphatically.

"You would hate getting wet and cold," Dad responded sensibly. "You know you take every snowflake as a personal affront. We could run into snow crossing the Rockies."

"I would have my helmet and my leather jacket. I would not complain."

"Yes, you would," replied Dad. "You would hate camping at the side of the road, night after night, in your little tent with a sleeping bag only partly dried out from the previous night's downpour."

"Well, I won't be in a tent. I plan to stay in a nice hotel every night. A hot shower, a meal in a fine restaurant, followed by a good night's sleep in a comfortable bed will make this a perfect holiday."

Dad did not really believe I was serious. He actually scoffed at the notion. I became the butt of many snide remarks and pointed

248

references to my preposterous notion of a holiday. But I was not joking. Perhaps this was the real me hiding under a veneer of ultra conservatism. But no one would ever know.

Until one momentous night, I opened my door to the sight of not one, but two motorcycles waiting outside. One had the unbelievable - a sidecar.

"Motorcycle Momma"

"But I could not get in it," I thought, pushing my walker nearer to have a good look. "Well, perhaps there would actually be room to stretch out my legs and get comfortable."

Soon Tom and Glen hoisted me up and I slipped into place.

"But first you need proper attire," Karen announced.

She had a collection of biker's clothes, and I chose a black leather jacket. Next was a long, flowing scarf and goggles. I suspect these goggles were actually for swimming, but what could I say? Topping this was a regulation helmet, perhaps a bit big, but nevertheless, effective. I looked just like the Red Baron, the famous WW2 Air Force Ace.

Then we were off, with the lead motorcycle breaking the way. Chelsea, Aaron's fiancée, was holding on to the driver and I, the Queen of the sidecar, was in my royal limousine.

I used my "Queen's" wave just like Elizabeth II, not wanting to tire my arm, as I saluted my lowly commoners, most of whom gave me curious glances.

"Just jealous," I said to my driver, as we whizzed by.

We had a smooth trip through Parksville. "This would be like crossing the Prairies," I thought.

Then we zoomed down the steep hill to the beach, mimicking the route through the Rockies. We even experienced some rough terrain as we bounced over the traffic bumps to the beach area. Then on to the ocean. We had experienced every road condition, in miniature, that Canada possesses.

Then we returned at the end of the long trip to a tasty snack and a soft bed in my own personal hotel just as I had envisioned.

Thanks for the memories.

Love,

Your Motor Cycle Momma.

The Family Tree – So Far

Family of Harry and Bessie McDonald

Harry Alexander McDonald
  b. 27 Jan 1907   Spokane, WA, USA
  d. 7 Aug 1993   Abbotsford, BC

Bessie Mae Pridmore
  b. 8 Nov 1905   Newark, Nott's, England
  d. 26 Dec 1980   Abbotsford, BC

Children
1. Mary Joyce McDonald

  b. 8 May 1930   Kisbey, SK

2. Ian Alexander McDonald
  b. 30 Jun 1931   Kisbey, SK
  Married Carmel Sottile
  Children: David, Michael, John

3. Donald Bain McDonald
  b. 10 Aug 1932   Abbotsford, BC
  Married Dianne Blacklock
  Children: Donald, Patricia, Richard

4. Michael McDonald
  b. 15 Sep 1934   Abbotsford, BC
  Married Ann Ogden
  Children: Michelle, Bruce

5. Ruth Diane McDonald
  b. 14 Sep 1936   Abbotsford, BC
  d. 2 Feb 2002   Victoria, BC
  Married Aubrey Brown
  Children: Michael, David, Cathy

Family of Fred and Rhoda Brown

Fred Brown
> b. 11 Feb 1892   Winchester, Dundas, ON
> d. 11 Nov 1964   Murrayville, Langley, BC

Rhoda Independence Flatt Hatch
> b. 04 Jul 1896   Grande Clariere, MB
> d. 15 Jun 1982   Burnaby, BC

Children
1. Herbert William Brown
   > b. 28 Mar 1917   Vancouver, BC
   > d. 04 Feb 1984   North Vancouver, BC
   > Married Hilda Garland
   > Children: Terry, Dennis, Paul

2. Lillian Hazel (Betty) Brown
   > b. 10 Oct 1918   Vancouver, BC
   > d. 31 Jan 2000   Quesnel, BC
   > Married Allen Woodrow Oakes (Sonny)
   > Children: Larry, Marilyn, Kenneth, Donald, Janet

3. George Fredrick Brown
   > b. 21 Oct 1922   Ocean Falls, BC
   > Married Ann Agnes (Nan) Simpson
   > Children: Evelyn, Heather

4. Teddy Raymond Brown

   > b. 8 May 1925   Ocean Falls, BC

   > d. 21 Sep 1998   Saskatoon, SK

5. Grace Mary Adele Brown
   > b. 3 Oct 1926   Vancouver, BC
   > Married William Pokeda, divorced
   > Children: Randy, Fred
   > Married George Hennessy

Family of Ted and Joyce Brown

Children
1. Catherine Diane Brown
   b. 15 Aug 1952   Langley Prairie, BC
   Spouse Lloyd Mark Rutledge, divorced

   Children
   1-1. James Alexander Rutledge
        b. 7 Jul 1981   North Vancouver, BC
   1-2. Sara Jane Rutledge
        b. 1 Dec 1982   North Vancouver, BC
   1-3. Karen Diane Rutledge
        b. 28 Feb 1985   North Vancouver, BC

   Step Children
   1-4. Marlie Suzanne Rutledge
        b. 28 Jul 1967   Prince George, BC
        Spouse Kelly Shane McCabe

        Children:
        1-4-1. Aleisha Nicole McCabe
               b. 24 May 1994   Prince George, BC
        1-4-2. James Brandon McCabe
               b. 13 Feb 1999   Vancouver, BC
        1-4-3. Kyle Stanley McCabe
               b. 27 Oct 2000 Prince George, BC

   1-5. Jeremy Ross Rutledge
        b. 24 Apr 1969   Fort St. John, BC
        Spouse Gail Denise Ferguson

        Step Child
        1-5-1. Tori Denise Barrett-Hewer
               b. 28 Nov 1992Surrey, BC
2. Thomas Frederic Brown
   b. 3 Jun 1954   Langley Prairie, BC
   Spouse Margaret Jean Zwack

   Children
   2-1. Gregory Duncan Brown
        b. 20 Apr 1983   Nanaimo, BC

2-2. Derek Cameron Brown
      b. 30 Jul 1984   Nanaimo, BC
2-3. Alexander David Brown
      b. 29 Oct 1987   Nanaimo, BC

3. David Allen Brown
    b. 29 Nov 1955   Langley Prairie, BC
    Spouse Elsie Rose Garr

    Children
    3-1. Joel Frederic Garr
        b. 16 Jun 1978   Ocean Falls, BC
        Spouse Christine Elizabeth Carter

        Child
        3-1-1 Asia Dene Rosa Carter Brown
            B 1 Oct 2004   Saskatoon, SK
        Step Child
        3-1-2. Aiden Nathaniel James Carter
            b. 12 Feb 1999   Saskatoon, SK
    3-2. Michael Justin Garr
        b. 22 Oct 1979   Ocean Falls, BC
    3-3. Alyson Megan Garr
        b. 23 Nov 1985   St. Albert, AB

    Spouse Melanie Trixie Laprise

    Children
    3-4. Alana Sarah Joyce Laprise
        b. 22 Oct 2002   La Loche, SK

    3-5. Alesha Laura Lynn Laprise
        b. 29 Nov 2003   Ft. McMurray, AB

    3-6 Ally Lexie Joy LaPrise
        b 6 June 2005   Ft. McMurray, AB

    Step Child
    3-7. Alex Arsene Carter
        b. 23 Nov 2000   Ft. McMurray, AB

4. Karen Rose Brown
   b. 7 Apr 1957   Penticton, BC
   Spouse Glen Robert Stranaghan

   Children:
   4-1. Crystal Jean Stranaghan
          b. 18 Jan 1979   Ocean Falls, BC
   4-2. Aaron James Stranaghan
          b. 27 Jul 1981   Nanaimo, BC
          Spouse Chelsea Hunt
   Child
   4-2-1 Cohen James Stranaghan
          b 15 July 2005   Nanaimo, BC
   Step Child
   4-2-2 Gavin McKeowen Titley
          b. 22 Aug 1999   Nanaimo, BC

5. Arlene Ruth Brown
   b. 10 Apr 1958   Matsqui, Abbotsford, BC
   Spouse William Frederick Veenhof

   Children
   5-1.William Nicholas Veenhof
          b. 6 Jan 1985   Rome, New York, USA
   5-2. Alysia Renee Veenhof
          b. 28 Sep 1986   North Bay ON
   5-3. Natasha Christine Veenhof
          b. 29 May 1990   Heerlen, Limburg,
Netherlands

6. Susan Marie Brown
   b. 13 Jan 1961   Langley Prairie, BC
   Spouse Nicholas Charles Jaques, separated

   Children
   6-1. Jessica Lauren Jaques
          b. 5 Feb 1987   North Vancouver, BC
   6-2. Cecilia Marie Jaques
          b. 10 Apr 1989   North Vancouver, BC

7. Mary Ann Cecilia Brown
   b. 20 Apr 1963   Bella Bella BC
   Spouse Robert John Herbert Wilson, divorced
   Spouse Gary Wayne Tennent

   Children
   7-1. Arlana Suzanne Tennent
      b. 7 Sep 1988   Victoria, BC

   Stepchildren
   7-2. Leah Michelle Tennent
      b. 15 Mar 1975   Victoria, BC
      Spouse Brian Bell
   7-3. Stefanie Annette Tennent
      b.18 Jan 1977   Victoria, BC

The Family Pictures

The Rutledge Family

Diane, Karen, Sara, James
James' Graduation RCMP -- January 19, 2004

The McCabe Family

Kelly & Marlie

Brandon, Aleisha
Kyle -- 2003

The Ross Rutledge Family

Gail, Ross
July 1998

Tori 2002

Gregory, Derek, Alex
Tom, Margaret
Christmas 2003

The David Brown Family

Michael, Melanie, David, Joel & Alana, Christine, Alyson
Alex, Aidan at Joel & Christine's Wedding - August 23, 2003

Ruth McKillop & Alesha
January 2004

Chelsea, Aaron, Karen, Glen, Crystal, Gavin
Aaron & Chelsea's wedding
February 19, 2004

Arlene, Nicholas, Bill
Aleisha, Natasha
Nicholas' Attestation Ceremony into
Canadian Armed Forces
June 2003

Cecilia, Jessica
Nick, Susan
August 2000

The Tennent Family

Arlana, Stephanie, Brian, Leah, Mary Ann Gary
Leah & Brian's wedding
August 19, 2000

August 23, 2003
Joel's wedding

ISBN 1-41205166-5

9 781412 051668